Democracy in Captivity

Democracy in Captivity

*Prisoners, Patients, and the Limits
of Self-Government*

Christopher D. Berk

UNIVERSITY OF CALIFORNIA PRESS

University of California Press
Oakland, California

© 2023 by Christopher D. Berk

Library of Congress Cataloging-in-Publication Data

Names: Berk, Christopher D., 1985– author.
Title: Democracy in captivity : prisoners, patients, and the limits of
  self-government / Christopher D. Berk.
Description: Oakland, California : University of California Press,
  [2023] | Includes bibliographical references and index.
Identifiers: LCCN 2022055942 (print) | LCCN 2022055943 (ebook) |
  ISBN 9780520394933 (cloth) | ISBN 9780520394940 (paperback) |
  ISBN 9780520394964 (ebook)
Subjects: LCSH: Prisoners—United States—Social conditions. |
  Democracy—United States. | Prisoners—Institutional care. |
  Prisoners—Civil rights—United States. | Criminals—Rehabilitation—
  United States.
Classification: LCC HV9469 .B468 2023 (print) | LCC HV9469 (ebook) |
  DDC 365/.973—dc23/eng/20230313
LC record available at https://lccn.loc.gov/2022055942
LC ebook record available at https://lccn.loc.gov/2022055943

32 31 30 29 28 27 26 25 24 23
10 9 8 7 6 5 4 3 2 1

Contents

Acknowledgments

No author stands alone. This work started its long journey, as most academic first books do, as a dissertation. Bernard Harcourt was the kind shepherd of that process. I couldn't have asked for a more generous mentor. He is the model of engaged scholarship that I can only hope to emulate. Cathy Cohen, Bob Gooding-Williams, and Andy Abbott brought not only their unique, genre-defying genius to our conversations, but tremendous patience. I feel privileged to have been their student.

I want to thank all of the friends, family, colleagues, library staff, and students (both on the outside and the inside) that took time out of their lives to offer research assistance, to suggest texts, to read drafts, to locate documents, to spitball over drinks or at the crag, to hunt for leads, to provide counsel, or simply to lend an ear. I can't hope to name you all. I ask those who are not mentioned here, but who contributed greatly, to forgive me for saying a private thank you next time we chat.

An earlier version of chapter 5 was published as "On Prison Democracy" in *Critical Inquiry* 44, no. 2 (2018). Thanks to the University of Chicago Press for permission to reprint this material. Without the help of Bobby Dellello and Jamie Bissonette Lewey, this project would never have gotten off the ground—they are the stewards of the Walpole Observer Program Files, which made that chapter possible to write. Joe Abrahams was generous with his time, both inviting me into his San Luis Obispo home and answering my long-winded questions about Howard

Hall over a number of phone calls. The chapter on St. Elizabeths is better for it. I am also grateful to Spencer Grant for permission to use his striking photograph on the cover of this book. All author royalties from this book will be donated directly to the Marshall Project.

This study could not have been conducted without sustained support across multiple universities. The Department of Political Science at the University of Chicago offered an intellectually rigorous and adventurous environment to begin my dissertation research. The Social Science Division provided both funding and, most importantly, time in the form of a Harper Fellowship in the later stages of graduate school. A year at the law school was illuminating and intellectually rejuvenating—thank you to Dave Weisbach for the opportunity to pursue a joint degree and to Tom Ginsburg for advising me in the MLS program. At the University of Virginia, Colin Bird and the program in political philosophy, policy, and law provided the ideal conditions to write the initial draft of this book. The Department of Politics and PPL funded a book workshop while I was a postdoctoral fellow that heavily influenced the form of the final manuscript. Heather Ann Thompson, Vesla Weaver, Bernard Harcourt, Stephen White, Lawrie Balfour, Jen Rubenstein, Claire McKinney, Matthias Brinkmann, and Manny Viedma all provided crucial input.

Portions of this book, and some closely related ideas, have been presented at many, many conferences and workshops over the years. While I can't list them all here, I'll single out the Political Theory Workshop at the University of Chicago and the PPL & Political Theory Colloquia at the University of Virginia as particularly significant. I thank all my colleagues in these places, faculty and students alike, for their hospitality and intellectual companionship.

It's been a pleasure to complete this book at the Schar School of Policy and Government at George Mason University. At Mason, I've found a university committed to intellectual inquiry and a department that treats its younger faculty as peers. Moses Hunsaker provided outstanding research assistance in the late stages of this project. Two anonymous reviewers for the University of Calfornia Press offered incisive feedback that has improved the book measurably. Maura Roessner, at the press, was enthusiastic and encouraging throughout the publication process.

I owe a different sort of debt to my teachers at the University of Washington. Naomi Murakawa, Jamie Mayerfeld, Michael McCann, Gary Segura, Glenn Mackin, David Watkins, and Christi Siver kindled my interest in these issues when I was a wide-eyed undergraduate. This project would not exist had I not been drawn into the profession by the examples they set.

Finally, if any people have left their imprint on this book it is my family. They are an everyday reminder of how grave an act it is to isolate someone from their loved ones. While too many have passed since this project began, I'm still marked by their unwavering faith and support. Their wisdom is woven into this book as their hearts are into my own. My grandmother, Hope Berk, and my father, Dimitri Berk, continue to be my biggest boosters. I can only hope others experience a fraction of the love they've shown to me. My uncle, Jim Nisbet, has been a trusted advisor over the years. And I cannot begin to measure my debt to Lyly—she always manages to keep perspective when mine is in danger of slipping away. Without her, I'm lost.

CHAPTER I

Custody and Democracy

Early nineteenth-century social reformers' understanding of the causes of deviant behavior led directly to the invention of mental asylums and modern prisons in the United States. The proper organization of custody, they believed, could address the specific influences that promote mental and social disorder. They turned their attention to the division of time and space within the institution: the layout of cell blocks, the methods of labor, the manner of eating and sleeping. External appearance and internal arrangement could both be designed to eliminate the circumstances that generate crime and model the fundamental principles of healthy community relations. Early advocates of asylums and prisons were responding not just to the disorder of Jacksonian America, as David Rothman notes in his classic text *The Discovery of the Asylum*, but to elements of modern democracy itself: expanded political participation, increased social mobility, and demands for intellectual and religious freedom. Prisons and mental hospitals offered a clear sense of order, discipline, and routine to counterbalance these unsettling transformations in social and economic life. Modern problems required a modern solution: custodial confinement.[1]

Less recognized, however, is that critics of custodial confinement held a similar faith. For a group of would-be democratic reformers, a repeated refrain was that a lack of participation and the absence of self-government were key causes of a number of maladies associated with prisons and mental hospitals, ranging from the spread of vice, to welfare

FIGURE 1. Prisoners at the library of the Norfolk Prison Colony, Norfolk, MA. Howard Gill founded the colony in 1927 with the idea of replacing traditional confinement with a shared democratic community that would serve as a "prison without bars." *Source:* Howard Gill Papers, John J. Burns Library, Boston College.

dependency, to inept facility management. Well-engineered opportunities for ward participation, such as town hall meetings and leadership councils, offered a potentially potent set of remedies. A participatory society was less an ethereal ideal to these thinkers and more a worldly governing strategy to bring order to disordered subjects. Democracy, they believed, was good therapy.

Reformers held an image of democracy *as* treatment and not, importantly, democracy *in* treatment. By the former term I mean the molding of ward participation—through voting, elections, deliberative fora, and other trappings of democratic politics—to secure and extend the authority of those already in power. By the latter I mean patients' and prisoners' ability to exert actual influence over the conditions of their confinement and care. This tension between *as* and *in* would linger when reformers attempted to put their ideas into practice.[2]

These democracy-minded reformers, and these ideas about participation, are not unique to any particular era. Each generation seems to discover them anew. We can find them at work in Thomas Osborne's Mutual Welfare League at Sing-Sing prison in the 1910s, which aimed to make "not good prisoners, but good citizens."[3] They can be found in the 1960s in patient power-sharing experiments at the Yale Psychiatric Institute, which attempted to "bridge the two worlds" of mental hospital treatment and the policy science of democracy.[4] At the turn of the twenty-first century they cropped up in "new-generation" facilities like the San Francisco county jail under the guise of therapeutic community.[5] Each generation produces its own democratic radicals and reformers. Each offers rallying cries of community control, odes to the therapeutic utility of self-government, and assertions of the superiority of participatory institutional design. Participatory schemes for correcting the deficiencies of citizens are, as Barbara Cruikshank suggests, endemic to liberal democratic societies.[6] The result is a reform tradition peppered with grand policy designs, social movements, and haphazard experiments.

The desire to democratize custody haunts both past and present reform efforts. And it's not hard to see why. On their face custodial arrangements appear to violate a commonly held intuition about political freedom as rooted in self-rule. That intuition holds that an individual or collectivity that is not self-governing is in some way subjugated, subordinated, or shackled by another. We're uncomfortable with paternalism. One generation's anxieties about custody echo into the next.

What should we make of these episodes and experiments in participatory governance? Where do wards and their custodians fit in a democratic political order? These questions are at the heart of this book. The answer offered here is that democracy has become inextricably bound to its shadowy underside of custodial confinement. The reformers who founded the modern penitentiary and asylum, along with those who have sought to democratize those same institutions, have in different ways tried to offer a decisive reply to the twin questions of who governs in custody and by what right. A key reason these reform visions, among others, remain unconvincing is a romanticism about civic competence. Reformers tend to separate their favored political theory of rule from the realities, ambivalences, and ambiguities of ward politics.

I argue that wards are not one-way migrants in or out of competence but are often positioned in between. As we'll see, the competence of wards to represent themselves is shaped by organizational contexts that at the same time are open to revision and tend to decay. Although typically unrecognized, these contexts are also critical sites of political contestation—contestation that invariably provokes backlash and repression. From the halls of St. Elizabeths Hospital in Washington, D.C., to the cell-blocks of the maximum security prison in Walpole, Massachusetts, backlash to wards struggling for representation needn't take the form of visible violence. It's not just the retaking of D Yard at Attica prison in New York State. Nor is it the scalpel of a surgeon severing tissue in a prefrontal cortex. It's not just the channeling of Black dissidents into asylums by diagnosing them with a "protest psychosis." Repression needn't don riot gear, use restraint chairs, or wield baton sticks. Of course, it certainly can. Repression wends its path through procedure: through adjusting who decides, how decisions are made, where those decisions take place, and the incentives for raising claims in the first place.[7] The result is not only the creation of pockets of authoritarianism, but the use of the language of "democracy" and "democratic management" to legitimatize those styles of rule.

We're held captive to this ebb and flow: the pressing needs of custody, the struggle for representation, and state repression. Given this cycle and the unique vulnerability of individuals in custody, we ought to think more broadly about how to stem the worst excesses of both custodians *and* aspiring reformers.

CUSTODIAL INSTITUTIONS

At first glance it might seem odd to treat prisons, mental hospitals, boarding schools, hospices, and so on under one heading: "custodial institutions." By using that term, I simply mean to suggest these institutions can be usefully classed together based on a series of structural similarities.[8] Most simply, prisons and asylums are formal organizations; they are defined by patterned, coordinated human decision-making aimed at achieving a series of ends. These ends might include therapy and rehabilitation, but they might also include objectives as basic as containment and incapacitation. For another, while organizations tasked with managing these populations vary in purpose (care, protection, punishment), each organization operates as parens patriae. Custodial organizations assume an authority analogous to that of a parent over a child. They assume custody, in the sense of public trusteeship. Finally, the authorization for that trusteeship is, at least in part, rooted in the belief that some individuals cannot, or ought not to, be full participants in economic, social, or political life.[9] Treating these organizations as a class, of course, necessarily papers over a variety of differences. The wager of the subsequent analysis is that this limitation will be outweighed by the value of unearthing patterns and phenomena otherwise obscured by treating them in isolation.

Similarly, instead of presupposing a set of givens about wards (about the nature of rationality, about mental illness, about criminality, about maturity, and so on) and then working out the consequences for politics, it's potentially more fruitful to flip the script.[10] We should act as if that universal given didn't exist and see how far we get. We might end up in a similar place, but we'd have a better account of how those assumptions work.

A full description of the similarities and differences of my approach in this book to others could lead us slogging through a semantic swamp. To avoid this detour, or to limit its length, I sketch a few observations here, without much in the way of a defense.[11]

Think of the contest to control wards' behavior as an ongoing, low-wattage battle. The conflict ebbs and flows, intensifies and fades; lines of movement are gained, then lost. Not only is there conflict between custodians, but there is also contention involving wards themselves. Far from being omnipotent rulers who have crushed all signs of rebellion, custodians are engaged in a continuous struggle to maintain the ideological order—and it is a struggle in which they frequently fail.[12] Wards resist the definition of their situation and, in more dramatic instances, attempt to supplant it through appeals to different normative orders, sometimes for the better, sometimes for the worse. Wards and custodians alike make claims about wards' interests, and this leads to individuals and collectives mobilizing on behalf of those interests.

This battle extends into the historical record. An archive catalogs evidence of these conflicts and is itself evidence of conflict. What artifacts and ephemera are included, and which are excluded, are the product of both human decisions and nondecisions.[13] Complicating matters is that the plausibility of any research depends on the grounds, the sources, from which the account is extracted and compiled. My response is to pull from both traditional state records and less traditional archives. Close readers will note that the narratives that follow are a pastiche of ward-authored (and institutionally censored) newspapers, handwritten notes of civilian observers, and autobiographical reflections of wards and custodians, among other alternative collections, in addition to more "official" records housed in government facilities. Each kind of evidence comes with its own challenges and its own opportunities.

With painstaking research this low-wattage battle for control is relatively straightforward to narrate but much more difficult to understand. Our analytical spade quickly hits bedrock. What's significant is not simply whether a particular movement or action was a success or a failure, but explaining how events so improbable became possible. At stake in that task is understanding political possibility in our own moment. To move the conversation about reform forward, we should look back. There is a pressing need to separate wheat from chaff, to parse practicable change from hallucinatory fantasies.

To that end, the chapters in the book treat the relationship between custody and democracy in three general registers. In the first register, the more micro histories I present chip away at a wider, macro understanding of custody. They collectively undermine the sway of what I refer to in the next chapter as *the exclusion thesis*. The tendency to think of custodial populations as bounded groups outside the scope of civil society, I argue, is rooted in a misdescription of the political world that ultimately has distributional consequences. Partitioning civil society in this way emboldens a kind of authoritarian managerialism in custody.

In my second register of analysis, we see the significance of narrative conflict. There is a link between narrative forms and forms of organization. It's not a straightforward assessment to describe a particular form of organization, custodial or otherwise, as more or less or democratic. Whether a particular institutional arrangement is recognized as democracy enhancing or detracting is a retrospective judgment that itself is a site of political struggle. The experiments, episodes, and (perhaps) lost causes revealed in the pages that follow highlight a shifting Overton window: the range of political ideas that a society is willing to countenance at a particular moment in time.[14]

Closest to the street, the third register of my analysis is organizational politics itself. While remaining agnostic about the virtue of any given form of custody, the normative project of deepening democratic commitments rests on the possibility of self-rule. I take seriously the timeworn dictum that *is* does not imply *ought*. That punishment, for example, tends to take a particular form doesn't mean that it should take that form. That certain avenues of participation are possible doesn't imply those avenues are desirable. And so on. However, even if is does not imply ought, ethicists are quick to point out that *ought* does imply *can*. If an ideal cannot work, or that ideal is incompatible with what we know is empirically possible, there is something dubious about prescribing that ideal.

Across these registers are prisoners and patients themselves. These are individuals caught up in institutions with a history aptly summarized, without hyperbole, as a chronicle of the depths of human suffering. Some of the ward organizers and advocates described in this book acted with great ability and acuity; this ability was at times deployed in ways that improved life and at others in tragic, self-defeating ways.

I want to avoid the temptation to gloss over the particularity and moral complexity of ward politics.[15] That temptation, as others have noted, is similar in kind to the impulse that segregated the sane from the insane, the upstanding from the deviant, in the first place.[16]

While notes on the registers just mentioned are present as a quiet melody throughout the history of custody, they become louder and more distinct during moments of conflict. The cases in this book leverage that fact. They reveal patterns, mechanisms, and relationships that are likely to be overlooked by studies that focus on routine practices across institutions or those that treat events such as the patient federation at St. Elizabeths Hospital (see chapter 3) and the rebellion at Walpole (see chapter 5) as rounding errors in an otherwise complete theory of democracy.[17]

Broadly, the orientation of this book is a general inductive skepticism. In taking that path, I am drawing on a rich set of traditions within democratic theory itself.[18] And like any inductive approach, it cannot be used to rule out the possibility that future evidence will contravene it. It couldn't be otherwise: if my account is to have any empirical footing, it also should be falsifiable.[19] I understand the analysis that follows to be exploratory. As a researcher, as a theorist, and as a writer, I've followed my own nose to places in the historical record that call out for closer examination. I leave it to my readers to assess my argumentative strategy. The proof of the pudding, after all, is in the eating.

ORGANIZATION OF THE BOOK

The rest of the book is organized as follows. When they are asked about the place of wards and their custodians in a democratic regime, one perspective dominates the contemporary commonsense reply among law and society scholars. That view focuses on the relationship between those in custody and the wider, outside public. What distinguishes the latter population from the former, we're told, is that those in custody, although citizens, are understood to be insufficiently self-governing and are rightfully subjected to paternal rule. As a result, one need not address the political situation of populations such as children, prisoners, or those with mental illness.

The problem with this view is not particularly philosophically intricate: it presupposes barriers to participation that either do not or need not exist. Or so I try to show in chapter 2. The assumptions that scaffold this view—what I call the *exclusion thesis*—are intuitive, but wrong. By misrepresenting the conditions necessary for participation, the exclusion thesis limits our imagination about the possibilities for change. Worse, as I suggest in the final chapter, it creates conditions that facilitate a creeping authoritarianism.

Chapters 3, 4, and 5 pull from the archives to sketch features of a wider reform tradition aimed at democratizing custodial confinement. In these key chapters I work inductively, from the warp and woof of the particular, and often peculiar, practices that constitute wards as agents to wider theoretical claims about custody and democracy.[20]

Chapter 3 presents the first historical case study of the book: St. Elizabeths Hospital, a midcentury asylum located in Washington, D.C. Between 1947 and 1965 the rise of therapeutic community approaches to mental health treatment produced an unintended by-product at St. Elizabeths Hospital: patient self-government. Over a few short years patients in Howard Hall, a maximum security ward for the "criminally insane," organized themselves; they came to collectively deliberate and advocate for policy changes at the hospital. I describe the politics of patient self-government at St. Elizabeths as caught in a strange kind of feedback loop. There was a generative relationship between the institutional processing of patient claims for voice and the democratic processing of the hospital itself. That is, patient participation was redirected and reshaped to shore up the interests of the hospital. At the same time, however, patients used group participation as a way to navigate their precarious existence. "Democracy as therapy" did more than simply alter the incentive structure for participation; it also shaped the identities, goals, and collective efficacy of wards.

The demise of patient self-government at St. Elizabeths is connected to a broader tradition of community control in custody. This is the focus of chapter 4. Participatory experiments in custody highlight the complex role organizations can play in making, and remaking, civic competence. Moreover, the failures of those projects in US prisons during the late 1960s and early 1970s can help us understand the limits and possibilities of custodial politics. Community control in custody, I contend, was at best an ameliorative, not transformative, political strategy. Prisoner participation was more shaped by, than shaped, the beliefs, institutional dynamics, and problem-solving tendencies of the institutions of which the prisoners were part. Principal among these shaping forces was the tendency to form a boundary around "incompetence," to locate its causes and solutions in the people who were experiencing those forces, and to interpret that incompetence in terms that did not require adjustment by those on the outside.

Chapter 5 examines a more grassroots vision of democracy in custody. In 1973 the prison officers at Walpole prison in Massachusetts went on strike. Walking away from their posts, officers assumed the prisoners would turn to violence in the absence of supervision. Instead, the prisoners organized a union, the National Prisoner Reform Association (NPRA), and administered the entire prison—without significant incident—for three months. Prisoners elected and organized a council, ran educational programs, and operated the foundry; they even adjudicated conflicts among prisoners and administered punishments. At stake in the rebellion was the fate of two clashing visions of self-rule, what I call the *divided* and *united* views of civil society. The latter view, offered by prisoners themselves, offered an alternative, radicalized vision of community control.

In a short concluding chapter I review key insights from earlier chapters and reflect on the normative implications of my study. I ask how one might imagine custodial arrangements that advance the normative project of self-government without repeating the errors of democratic reformers and without succumbing to what I describe in earlier chapters as a "false belief in necessity." Organizational practices do political work on the agents that perform them, with often ambiguous results. Bringing attention to those practices might put us in a better place to make more sensitive judgments about if and how, precisely, custody ought to be organized. The final pages forward the claim that we ought to think more broadly about publicity in custody. By publicity I mean the institutional mechanisms and policies that bring the actions of officials before the general public for examination and evaluation.

While that chapter concludes the book, I don't see it as a conclusion. Motivating the study that follows is a suspicion that there is a fundamental incoherence underlying our understanding of democratic participation: a vision of voice and inclusion that we will not give up partly because it is essential to the way in which we make sense of our world. To understand how custody might be otherwise, we need to hold the feet of that vision to the fire, not to destroy, deform, or discount it, but to bring its promises and dangers out of the shadows.

CHAPTER 2

Patients, Prisoners, Children, and Travelers

"The demos must include all adult members except transients and mental defectives."[1] The *exclusion thesis* asserted here by Robert Dahl is so common, so self-evident, that it seems its only being mentioned is enough to persuade. Jane Mansbridge echoes, "One obvious exception . . . is the case where individuals do not know their interests as clearly as someone else does. We habitually make this assumption, for example, about children and the mentally ill."[2] Benjamin Barber adds lawbreakers to the list of exceptions: "Criminals, as criminals, forfeit their citizenship because . . . they have ceased to engage in talk, deliberation, and common action and have substituted private force for public thinking."[3] Those we put into schools, mental hospitals, and prisons are *custodial* populations; they are individuals understood to be insufficiently self-governing and, consequently, rightfully disqualified in part or whole from participation in civic life.[4] They lack maturity (the child), lack rationality (the "mad"), or lack sociality (the "criminal")—all qualities that are intuitively necessary to decide, deliberate, or participate in the polity.[5]

However, the political situation of wards is much more complex than the glib references to exclusion just surveyed would imply. Disqualification, for one, is not all or nothing. As a number of legal theorists have noted, the "braid" of various rights in liberal democratic regimes is, in practice, unbundled.[6] For another, political struggle constantly passes through institutional walls. The largest prison work strike in US history, after all, was less than a decade ago.

FIGURE 2. The Howard Hall building at St. Elizabeths Hospital, in Washington, DC. This facility housed men facing criminal charges found to be non compos mentis; those who had attacked other patients or staff; and in 1947, those admitted under the sex psychopath statute. *Source:* Record Group 418-P (Box 4), National Archives and Records Administration in College Park, MD.

Nonetheless, the exclusion thesis continues to shape the imagination of would-be reformers. In the following I suggest the exclusion thesis is not one claim but a multiplicity masquerading as one. When the exclusion thesis is taken to be a conceptual claim about the limits of democratic participation, I argue that it simply doesn't stand to reason. Even if internal "borders" around competence are necessary to a particular conception of democracy, those boundaries are porous and ineluctably contestable.[7] I make the case here that the exclusion thesis illuminates certain aspects of democratic life while, or by, obscuring others. Naomi Murakawa and Katherine Beckett describe how a "penology of racial innocence" can erase the exercise of racial power; similarly, the way custody is mentally mapped in democratic thought can constrain what scholars have come to call our "carceral imagination."[8] The exclusion thesis widens the gap between the complexity of our empirical studies of custody and the simplicity of our collective normative reasoning about custody.

This chapter is composed of two complementary parts. One is diagnostic, the other reconstructive. In the initial, diagnostic, part, I place the exclusion thesis in a wider debate in democratic theory about how to constitute the demos. I start by sketching the idea of "democratic exclusions." Unlike ascriptive exclusions, the exclusion of patients and prisoners has a more intimate connection to the ideal of self-rule that animates modern democratic politics. The exclusion thesis shares a structural resemblance to what contemporary theorists describe as the "democratic boundary problem," and I suggest that this similarity offers an inroad into understanding the place of participation in custody. In the latter, reconstructive, part of this chapter, I suggest that the anxiety about self-rule at the heart of the politics of custody taps an important truth. Instead of thinking about those in custody as incapable or capable of political voice, we should instead see competence as a shifting and fluid limit to which institutions respond and adapt. For some, my claims about exclusion are intuitive and an excursion into more abstract democratic theory to defend them is an unwanted detour. To these readers I simply beg your patience; alternatively, I invite you to skip to the final two sections of this chapter.

DEMOCRATIC EXCLUSIONS

The situations of prisoners and the mad are usually taken to be paradigmatic cases of formal exclusion, even civil death.[9] Zimring, for example, counts at least 44,605 "civil disabilities" imposed in the United States on persons with criminal conviction records. These range from restrictions on the right to vote to restrictions on being employed as a barber or beautician.[10] Likewise, entire classes of citizens with intellectual disabilities are disqualified from the franchise.[11] Civic disqualifications are often justified as a needed compromise among competing aims or grounds—instrumental grounds like public health during a pandemic, for example, or intrinsic grounds like moral deserts. A democratic "loss" is brooked for the sake of other, more compelling interests.[12] Vitally, the weight of the belief that there *is* a trade-off acts as a backstop to a more general erosion of rights. The grounds on which wards are disqualified are, however, potentially a bit more peculiar. It's not clear that disqualification is always seen as a compromise or as a tragic choice. Whether in part or in full, the civic exclusion of wards is typically seen as either neutral or democracy enhancing.

While the institutional prescriptions of aggregative, deliberative, and participatory democrats vary, major authors in each tradition mark out custodial populations having a special and unequal status. Aggregative democrats tend to treat the individual as the best authority on her own interests and seek to organize the polity along the lines of expressed or revealed preference. Some individuals, however, are thought not to know their interests and are placed under a form of liberal guardianship. Deliberative theorists have a more demanding set of prescriptions for democratic institutions. What distinguishes noise from speech in deliberative contexts is the presumption that interlocutors are autonomous and reasonable. Children, to take another interesting case, fail to meet these standards and need to be gradually introduced to the discursive community.[13] Participatory democrats offer the most demanding vision of the polity, calling for the democratization of almost all spheres of life. For Barber, the limits of calls for universal inclusion are clear: "Even those who most zealously honor the principle of universality find themselves bending the abstract boundaries of the biological species when dealing with the civic role of children, criminals, the insane, and foreigners."[14] Children are potential citizens, as are criminals; full citizenship lies in wait for each group to acquire the ability or will to claim their civic rights. Until that time, surrogacy is the appropriate means of providing representation.[15]

In each philosophical tradition the aim of universal democratic inclusion is tempered by competence. Commenting on the intellectual history of human rights, Jennifer Pitts notes that "universalisms always take a particular form, with respect to the metaphysical framework in which universal claims are made as well as the anthropological qualities asserted to be universally human."[16] Childhood, madness, and criminality cast in relief these particular conceptual features, acting as edge cases for claims about the nature of political personhood and competence in theories of democracy. The "half-hidden premises, unexplored assumptions, and unacknowledged antecedents" of a given universalism form a "vaguely perceived shadow theory that forever dogs the footsteps of explicit, public theories of democracy."[17]

What does exclusion in the "shadow theory" of democratic citizenship look like? To start, exclusions in democratic polities can be broad. The historical record is replete with examples of the exclusion of racial and ethnic minorities, women, and those who hold views anathema to the founding national myths, among others. The prevalence of exclusions reflects the tendency of democracies to disqualify from a full schedule of rights those who can't or won't fit into the mold of the popular majority.[18] In one formulation, these kinds of exclusions are simply mile markers on the path to total inclusion. A less optimistic interpretation is that these exclusions persist because they take the form of a "wicked" policy problem and often require large (even generational) shifts in attitudes to solve.[19]

That said, the exclusions of the mad and prisoners are democratic exclusions in multiple senses of the word *democratic*.[20] For one, the disqualification of these populations is the product of a particular liberal-democratic project. Under a monarch, for example, everyone—mad or sane, child or adult—is equally subject to the crown. The modern doctrine of legitimacy based on consent introduced the link between competence and inclusion. For another, these are disqualifications agreed upon, or legitimated by, democratic procedures. In other words, these groups are excluded by tacit or explicit majorities. And finally, they are democratic exclusions in the sense that each group is understood to be unable or unwilling to meet the basic conditions for democratic participation. In sum, the exclusion thesis is a weave of claims about democratic provenance, democratic procedure, and democratic principle.[21]

These claims, in turn, contain a mix of empirical and conceptual propositions. A confusion of intuitions and conclusions creates a bundle of implicit premises that need to be pried apart. Emphasizing provenance and procedure, exclusion appears as historically and culturally contingent. Different origins, for example, might mean that an otherwise disqualified group (custodial or otherwise) is enfranchised. The same is the case with procedure. A different majority or different set of laws might lead the boundary line dividing competence from incompetence to be drawn differently. One could imagine, for instance, allowing young children to participate in municipal budgeting.[22] Alternatively, the mechanism behind exclusion could be *cohesion*, the idea that custodial populations cannot be assimilated (unreformed, uneducated, or unhealed) without harming the identity of the wider demos. Here, again, one can imagine a counterfactual wherein institutional innovations channel the force of cohesion toward greater inclusion. Provenance and procedure invite a discussion of historical and empirical possibilities but don't provide a compelling normative reason to treat custodial populations as different in kind from ascriptive exclusions.

The exclusion thesis, I suspect, is rooted in a deeper claim concerning principle. The sensitivity to "non-sovereignty," "relationality," and "vulnerability" in the outer, social world tends not to be extended to the inner world of competence. Modern theorists of democracy tend to define competence *prepolitically* when it comes to the scope of the demos.[23] By "prepolitical" I mean boundaries are understood to be formed prior to the public sphere through essentially private or natural means such as biology, culture, or even personal choice.[24]

Importantly, ascriptive exclusions like racism also can function prepolitically. What distinguishes racism from the exclusion thesis is that the former presents a *historical* dilemma for inclusion, while the latter potentially creates a conceptual one. As Joel Olson writes, "The dilemma between *inclusion and participation* is a historical consequence of racialized citizenship in the United States, not an inherent contradiction."[25]

In contrast, custody is traditionally taken to be "prior, both causally and constitutively to the exercise of political power."[26] Custody is causal in the sense that categories like child, mad, and criminal are not merely the products of laws and institutions but arise directly from the actual features of members of that population. And it is prepolitical in the constitutive sense insofar as members are understood to share some set of properties that do not amount to being subject to the same political institutions, or to its having been decided, by authoritative political procedures, that they share the same properties.[27]

One might balk at applying this line of reasoning to prisoners. To be sure, whether prisoners fit into this account of custody depends in no small part on the theory of punishment one embraces. For example, one could reasonably argue that those convicted of a crime are excluded as a matter of *deserts*, not competence or capacity. Fair enough. However, even in systems that are nominally rooted in strict retributive principles, questions of competence and character still linger. Assessments of "dangerousness" are integral to the functioning of contemporary penal law—from bail, to sentencing, to housing classification, to parole, to the civil disabilities cataloged by Zimring mentioned previously. This kind of assessment, at least in theory, works on a register separate from political concerns about distributive justice or judgements about blameworthiness.[28] Furthermore, arguments about moral desert do a poor job of explaining or justifying practices like felon disenfranchisement.[29] Even so, the intuition that custody is grounded in a set of "prepolitical" assumptions is probably strongest for children and weakest for prisoners.

Dahl recognizes the difficulties that competence creates for a theory of democracy. However thoughtful his vision of democratic life, he treats the core values of democracy—"intrinsic equal worth," for instance— as an engineer would. He takes the social system as given, accepts its account of itself, and develops a normative theory with an eye toward helping society achieve what it claims to value given those facts. Something similar obtains in the participatory democratic tradition. Barber, like Dahl, acknowledges the ambiguities around the borders of citizenship. In aggregative democracy, he writes, boundaries are a function of agreement and thus a matter of contract, of what we *agree* to. In unitary systems it's a matter of identity, of who or what we *are*. And in "strong" participatory democracy, boundaries are a function of activity, of what we *do*. In this last form, Barber's participatory approach, the scope of citizenship itself becomes a subject of ongoing discussion and review, "and one's participation in such discussion becomes a brief for inclusion."[30] However, to avoid exclusion by the vagaries of power, Barber backs down from rejecting prepolitical foundations entirely. "If the idea of open citizenship is not to become a one-way door through which undesirables are continuously ejected, it must be conditioned by the premise of biological universality." As with Dahl, this premise underscores a need to separate claims about personhood from claims about the proper domain of participatory democratic politics. Underneath a diversity of ontological assumptions, for which Dahl and Barber are representative, democratic theorists tend to share a single imagination about the place of competence in democratic life.

The prepolitical claim about democratic exclusion does a lot of intellectual work. It's not simply that it squares authoritarian forms of governance with otherwise democratically organized societies, though we'll see in subsequent chapters that's often the case. The prepolitical claim facilitates large-scale, often radical interventions into human lives—"authoritarian," "participatory," or otherwise. The history of custodial efforts like psychiatric care, colonialism, and moral reform that shuttled people into custodial institutions like asylums, reservations, and industrial schools offers a series of unsettling case studies. By creating and reinforcing a categorical division between an arena for democratic, self-governing citizens and a domain where paternalism is necessary, appropriate, and effective, the exclusion thesis insulates the design of contemporary institutions like prisons, hospitals, and schools from significant lines of criticism—particularly when that criticism is voiced by wards themselves.[31]

Even when wards explicitly protest their situation, for example, they are still not part of the demos. Consider the situation of children. While there is no one view of childhood that emerges from the liberal tradition, there is a general shared intuition that childhood constitutes a special status, and that status has a dual character. On the one hand, children are in need of protection; they are dependent on others for their basic care, and they need time to experience, learn, and play without facing serious consequences for their choices. On the other, this means children live under a form of guardianship in which their voices and actions have only consultative value. The crux of the liberal paternal intuition is that children cannot fully consent, yet they can justly be assimilated into the liberal polity. Put simply, "present compulsion is a precondition of subsequent choice."[32] Similar arguments are made in the context of cognitive disability and imprisonment: "Given the lawless and uncivilized character of their citizens, inmate societies ought . . . to be subject to strong official controls and a tight, mandatory regime of work and programs."[33] The claims of wards, when heard, are simply data to be interpreted by others.

There is a series of propositions the exclusion thesis does *not* imply. For one, exclusion does not imply abandonment. Tremendous amounts of resources are marshaled to *include* custodial populations into the polity. The outside public—that is, those who are not in custody—is tasked with securing basic interests of wards. A "special status" is assigned (prisoner, patient), and a particular set of institutions is tasked with realizing the general obligations associated with that status.[34] Ian Shapiro describes the relationship as fiduciary; representatives of the state hold a ward's rights of democratic citizenship in trust until he, she, or they are cured, educated, or rehabilitated.[35] For another, exclusion needn't be all or nothing. The "braid of citizenship rights" is in practice unwoven in liberal democracies.[36]

One might think that institutions with wards that have little voice in the conditions of their lives would, on the face of it, be incompatible with the demands of constitutional democracy. However, an extension of the exclusion thesis is that the reference "public" that holds custodians democratically accountable is *outside* institutional walls; consequently, there is no democratic deficit created by (for instance) authoritarian forms of custody, care, or schooling. However, as we'll see, the question of who is or is not a member of the public is not so easily settled.

CONSTITUTING THE DEMOS

Attentive readers will notice that in the preceding brief survey of modern democratic theorists I glossed over the group traditionally used to mark the boundaries of the demos: travelers. Dahl, you'll recall, mentioned *transients* in the same breath as "mental defectives." Likewise, Barber referred to the "civic role of children, criminals, the insane, and *foreigners*." Travelers are neither full citizens nor noncitizens; they are situated in between. While it's less clear what's owed to this group, there are a number of well-accepted rights, duties, and limits in the exercise of state power.[37] Travelers have access to some of the rights of citizenship (e.g., access to criminal courts) but not others (say, parliamentary elections).

The analogy to custodial populations is relatively straightforward. A democracy's external borders, it is implied, have some relation to its internal borders. In the following I take this analogy seriously, pushing it to its limit on its own terms, with the aim of seeing how far we can get. I argue that the exclusion thesis described in the previous section, understood as a kind of claim about sovereign boundaries, runs smack into what some political philosophers have termed the "boundary problem."[38]

Shapiro and Casiano Hacker-Cordón put it bluntly: "An enduring embarrassment of democratic theory is that it seems impotent when faced with questions about its own scope."[39] That is, there are no clear answers about who should be included or excluded in a democratic decision-making process. "We the people" is a deceptively simple formula for democratic rule. "Before the people can decide, one must first decide who are the people." This "boundary problem" and related paradoxes of democratic governance have been the object of sustained analysis for contemporary democratic theory.[40] While most of the debate has centered on migration across *territorial* borders, thinking of the boundary problem spatially obscures more than it clarifies. I prefer Robert Goodin's redescription of the boundary problem as a problem of "constituting the demos."[41] Questions of membership need not involve literal borders, as I detail later.

How to constitute the demos is not a peripheral problem, nor is it simply a question of how to found a polity. As a number of scholars have highlighted, simply accepting the way a particular demos has constituted itself as morally or politically neutral commits one to both implausible and undesirable outcomes.[42] Defining membership is a paradigmatic instance of the exercise of political power; to place it outside the scope of democratic theory is, in effect, to overlook a kind of theft.[43] Moreover, every time a decision is made or a law is enacted, the problem of how to constitute the demos rears its head.[44] A law is legitimate only insofar as it refers back to the persons over whom power is exercised. Democratic legitimacy is inextricably tied to the borders of membership.[45]

If one cannot safely ignore the significance of how the demos is constituted (for the sake of coherence or for the sake of preserving a normatively defensible vision of democratic governance), then normative theorists who embrace this imagined cartography of custody are faced with three main options: advocate open borders, abandon a total theory of democracy, or seek out a democratic principle to justify a given boundary. In the context of international migration and nation-states, those concerned with recognizing cultural identity and diversity find the first option incoherent, and committed cosmopolitans abhor the defeatism of the second.[46] Most academic debate over the last decade on territorial borders has centered on the third option, finding a set of principles internal to democratic theory by which a particular border regime can be justified.

The two principles that serve as lodestars in the debate are the "all-affected interests" principle and the more circumscribed "subjection" principle. The former principle is inspired by Robert Dahl, the latter by theorists of autonomy like Joseph Raz. Rather than ask what institutions ought to exist, interlocutors in this debate reverse the question of legitimacy. Given a particular immigration policy—say, for example, the institutions that regulate migration across the US-Mexico border—what is necessary to secure legitimacy? That is, given that a border stands in need of some justification, what would be required to secure that justification? This form of "institutional theorizing" about borders has led to a productive debate about who, precisely, is owed such justifications.[47] Is the mere presence of a wall along a border coercive?[48] Who, precisely, is affected by the decision to burn coal for fuel?[49]

These questions, however, don't appear to admit of a clear and uncontroversial answer. David Miller provides a persuasive explanation for the persistence of controversy. For Miller, ideals of democracy are caught between an inclusionary push (liberalism, the centrifugal extension of rights) and an exclusionary pull (republicanism, the centripetal forces of cohesion and solidarity). He writes:

> My question has been whether democratic theory itself can give us an answer to the question of democracy's domain, and my answer to it is that we must strike a balance between the need to have a demos that functions well internally and the need to include within the demos those whose lives will be systematically impacted by its decisions. . . . These are difficult questions to answer. Because trade-offs are involved, there can be no algorithm for deciding whether any proposed shift of domain represents a democratic gain or a democratic loss. For the same reason, we should not think that domain

questions can be resolved through the rulings of some external committee of experts. Instead they are questions that must be debated within existing demoi whenever proposals for altering boundaries appear on the agenda.[50]

Every demos has a particular conception of democracy, and that particular conception will impact whether a given reconstitution of the demos produces a democratic gain or loss.

This concern, of course, needn't enter the conversation about custody if exclusions are (as noted in the previous section) taken to be prepolitical. For some, like Claudio López-Guerra, a weak competency criterion (what he calls the "franchise capacity") is the only way to provide a philosophically sound justification for the electoral exclusions of young children and those with profound cognitive disabilities.[51] Here, too, the discussions of the borders of the nation-state can trouble the intuitions of the exclusion thesis. Arash Abizadeh argues that appeals to a prepolitical "nation" to ground the demos face a problem of closure, "the problem that neither specifying the putative boundaries of *cultural groups* (which individuals?) nor specifying those of cultures themselves (what criteria?) admit[s] of determinate answers."[52] In any given feature that might assign membership to the group—shared history, shared language, shared values, shared ethnicity—there is no clear bright line to delimit membership. To say that the problem of closure exists is not to say that a category is simply or strictly a product of social convention or prejudice. Nor is it to say fuzzy boundaries imply the absence of a difference in kind.[53] What closure means is that there is not a decisive criterion for membership; that the line marking the category is essentially (and intractably) contested; and that the demos is, in Abizadeh's terms, necessarily *unbounded*.

What is true of culture, I argue, is also true of custody. The categories that we currently use to define the life course—infancy, child, adolescence, youth, adult—don't admit of clean borders; vary by culture and context; and are the product of particular, and at times peculiar, histories.[54] Likewise with madness. The history of the *Diagnostic and Statistical Manual of Mental Disorders* (DSM) gives a sense of the difficulties and uncertainties endemic to psychiatric classification.[55] Moreover, much ink has been spilled on historical continuities and discontinuities in defining crime and criminality.[56] Custodial populations are invariably hybrid. Madness bleeds into sanity, youth into adulthood, criminal into lawful. And even small shifts in definition can have a significant impact on disqualification or enfranchisement.[57]

As a consequence, some sort of external "supplement" is needed to anchor the boundaries of the demos.[58] In the case of custody, that supplement is usually a particular system of professional knowledge—psychiatry, criminology, developmental psychology—or a cultural script—collective beliefs about the transition to adulthood, for example.[59]

The need for a supplement highlights how competence is a social, not natural, fact. In contradistinction to natural facts, social facts cannot be reduced to the sheer physical attributes of the object in question. Social facts are characterized by the collective assignment of functions to phenomena—the attribution of a status—that is both nonphysical and noncausal.[60] Again, this is not to say that social facts are entirely "made up." Observer-independent features of the world can and do condition the attribution of a status to an object. It's just that the physical features of the object do not determine or exhaust the content of the fact.[61]

While these debates in the philosophy of borders, citizenship, and migration are not settled, they are suggestive. Bringing the strands of argument together, the exclusion thesis faces two key difficulties. The first is evaluative: that claims about democratic gains and losses are necessarily internal to a particular conception of self and democracy.[62] The second is conceptual: that the boundaries around the categories of criminal, mad, and child are necessarily porous.[63] As a consequence, potentially all practices of exclusion based on competence are open to contest, resignification, and deinstitutionalization. In the place of the exclusion thesis we're left with an absence, a line of inquiry, not a set of answers: an inquiry into the forms of democracy proper to a world in which the boundaries of the demos are in flux.

BEYOND BORDER POLITICS

The larger problem I have outlined is something like *fixity*, the tendency for existing arrangements to consolidate around a given border or set of categories. The analogy to migration admittedly obscures as much as it clarifies; wards are not one-way migrants in or out of competence, but are often positioned in between.[64] Fixity, however, cuts both ways. Its absence allows nonstandard claims for participation to appear on the agenda, yet its presence is a requisite for any meaningful claims making. There must be some authority, in the final analysis, that makes binding decisions on membership.[65]

To successfully navigate this narrow path, the question traditionally asked about competence ought to be flipped. Instead of asking about entry and exit from the category "competent citizen" (under what conditions is someone rightfully labeled mad; what legal or moral criteria ought to be used to assess maturity), we should ask what it means to be a self-governing individual in a society where individuals are constantly entering and exiting the category of competence, in a society wherein well over 90 percent of those currently in prison will be released, children can be tried as adults, and cognitive disability at some point in the life course is an expectation, not an exception.

The standard replies to this flipped question only get us so far. Include everyone. Collectively determine the boundaries of the demos. Turn to science to define limits of competence. Invoke criteria from moral philosophy to establish the conditions for enfranchisement. Each of these, we have seen, fails in particular ways to give a compelling reply that respects the intuition behind self-rule, the desire for democratic legitimacy, and the very real need for custodial care.

What's needed is not closure but a recognition that the borders of custody are defined by a kind of provisional agreement that is subject to question, possible suspension, and, as a consequence, is open to future contest. The model of self-government implied by the exclusion thesis is one in which a straight line can be drawn between competence and participation. This is an unwarranted and unhelpful distortion. As we'll see over the next few chapters, custodial organizations, by accident or by design, stymie, distort, authorize, recombine, translate, and amplify the competence to represent one's own interests in public.

One might object, however, that this perspective may be empirically tractable but is normatively suspect. *Is* does not imply *ought*, after all. There is a clear problem with embracing a world wherein the boundary of civil society is up for grabs; the inertia in a given system is not, by necessity, toward greater inclusivity or greater autonomy. Unlike the exclusion thesis, there is little to shore up its borders; it might in fact entail a more closed institution than one premised on another criterion—for instance, Barber's "biological humanity" or López-Guerra's "franchise capacity." And even if a meaningful normative account is available, critics may argue, that account is too open to "identify with satisfactory precision the specific groups of people who should or may legitimately be disenfranchised according to the democratic tradition."[66] Without another value, without some anchor in a value like freedom or autonomy, one might wonder why focusing on competence as a provisional political settlement is a useful starting point.

To offer a convincing response to this objection, it's helpful to reflect on the structure of my argument as a whole. Using the analogy to sovereign borders, I started by describing how the demand for voice by those in custody is entangled in a meta-disagreement about how to constitute the demos, then offered a corresponding premise that can accommodate this sort of disagreement. What's needed is not closure, I have suggested, but an account that focuses on competence as a kind of social settlement that is subject to future revision.

This means that yes, at one time the number of participants or avenues of participation in a polity may contract, and at another time they might expand. The desire for definitive measurement, for clear borders, draws us in because it is an effective means to ease our own anxiety.[67] What might be read as intellectual modesty has decidedly immodest implications. Rather than being given all at once, dimensions of justice are disclosed historically, through the medium of social struggle.[68] The process of claims making is an open-ended experiment that requires epistemic humility.

To be clear, none of this is to deny the reality of actual exclusion, incompetence, and dependence. It is a demonstrable fact that the demos *is* often constituted in precisely the ways aggregative, deliberative, and participatory democratic theorists mentioned at the start of this chapter describe. And there are a variety of empirical reasons why the demos is (or ought to be) drawn to exclude these groups—at least under existing social conditions.[69] However, by collapsing conceptual limits into empirical limits we're left with an imagination constraining *misdescription.*[70] It's a difference in kind between saying "the mad cannot participate," as if we were confronted with a conceptual limit, and the more careful judgment that the mad cannot participate for contingent, empirical reasons. The former reifies the socially generated dynamics that, by reference to ideal and actually existing alternatives, political theory and social science ought to question.[71]

DEMOCRACY IN CUSTODY

Custodial institutions, and the idea of parens patriae, have been the main way liberal democratic societies have managed the worst off among their citizens, and the exclusion thesis has, often implicitly, justified broad forms of civic disqualification.[72] Partitioning the political world, I've suggested, emboldens a kind of authoritarian managerialism in custody that erases concerns over self-rule. The same is true, ironically, of the democratic reformers we follow over the next few chapters. Rather than simply erase concerns over self-rule, they displaced them.

Reformers, to various degrees, embraced prefigurative politics: the idea that the organizational form a group takes should embody the kind of society they wish to create. However appealing this vision, it runs the risk of treating the transformation of desire as a disciplinary project— that is, a project to willfully alter the desires of wards in line with a particular view of the political world. Worse, as we see in chapter 4, this approach allows its adherents to substitute local change for collective transformation.[73]

At the heart of reformers' efforts was an unease about who ought to govern ward life. Their attempts to soothe that apprehension provide a unique window into the various techniques used to redefine, resist, and remix accepted ideas about democratic citizenship. At St. Elizabeths Hospital, where we turn next, this expressed itself as an equivocation between democracy *in* therapy and democracy *as* therapy. Hidden in the space between *in* and *as* is a whole domain of struggle on the ward and in the cellblock. Without the comfort of the exclusion thesis, a different sort of democratic politics comes into focus.

CHAPTER 3

Mad Politics

Consider two visions of ward self-government. The first comes from a gushing *Harper's* feature on St. Elizabeths in 1956 for the hospital's centennial:

> When [the patient] was admitted to Howard Hall, the walled maximum-security building for the criminally insane, he expected cells, rifles, side arms, perhaps clubs and blackjacks. Instead he was escorted to his ward by a fellow patient, introduced around, and given a tour of the building. He saw patients working in a shop (one of them taking a correspondence course to learn how to be a radio mechanic), editing a newspaper, playing softball and badminton, even pitching horseshoes; he heard a patient orchestra practicing; he was told that there was patient self-government in Howard Hall, and almost no attempts at escape.[1]

At roughly the same time, Erving Goffman was conducting ethnographic fieldwork that would culminate in *Asylums: Essays on the Social Situation of Mental Patients and Other Inmates*.[2] Goffman writes:

> Although house organs [patient newspapers, official publications] have been customary for some time, it is only recently that a somewhat similar form of role release has appeared in total institutions; I refer here to the several forms of "self-government" and "group therapy." Typically, the inmates speak the lines and a congenial member of the staff performs the supervision. . . . The inmates are given the privilege of spending some time in a relatively "unstructured" or equalitarian milieu, and even the right to voice complaints. In return they are expected to become less loyal to the countermores and more receptive to the ideal-for-self that the staff defines for them.[3]

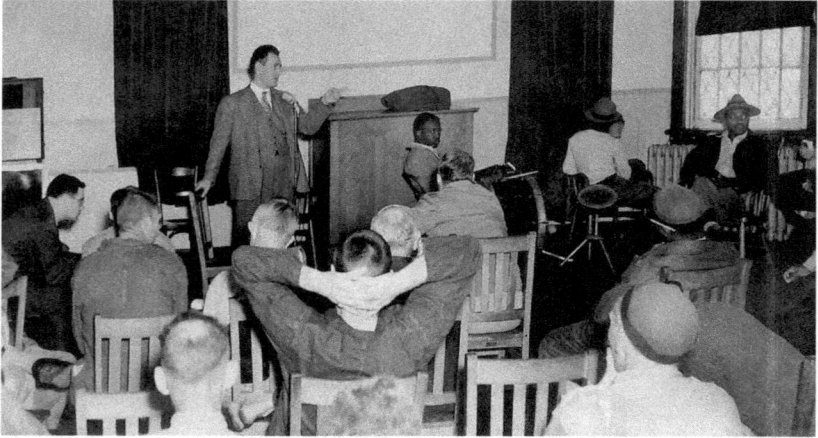

FIGURE 3. Dr. Joseph Abrahams addressing the patients of Howard Hall at St. Elizabeths Hospital in 1947. *Source*: Personal collection of Joseph and Elisabeth Abrahams.

On the one hand, we have a vision of a community, a small city of the mad. This vision, the official line at the time, is one in which patients learn to be capable citizens through opportunities for self development, whether through work, play, or participation in organizational management. On the other, we have a vision of self-government as an insidious extension of totalitarian rule, a means of turning patients against each other and against themselves. Between these two accounts the object itself—the practice of patient self-government—is largely lost to contemporary discussions of democratic politics.

PATIENT SELF-GOVERNMENT

The mad are often taken to be irrational, dangerous, or even otherworldly; objects of pity, care, or concern, but not, in most accounts, the proper subjects of democratic institutions.[4] But the reality of asylum life suggests a more complex picture. Patients can be sophisticated participants in the institutions tasked with their confinement and care.

The basic architecture of legal rights for patients committed to mental hospitals that we know today didn't emerge until the 1960s and 1970s.[5] Before that time, patients had little recourse to the courts to address intolerable hospital conditions or to protect their due process rights.[6] For those found incompetent to stand trial, like many of the residents of Howard Hall described later, the situation was particularly bleak; even if patients were judged to be of sound mind, they would immediately face a criminal trial or plea deal, then be shuttled off to prison. Despite the inability to make a cognizable legal claim, and despite significant collective action problems—the ubiquitous potential for ward conflict, staff and patient predation, various and sundry illnesses—patients could, and did, collectively advocate for better ward conditions. How did "the mutterers, the masturbators, and the paranoid" of Howard Hall accomplish such a feat?

To become participants in the hospital order, patients required mechanisms to test reality, resolve conflict, and represent their interests. In this chapter I detail two sets of institutions that patients and staff devised for this purpose. The first set was an outgrowth of group psychotherapy. An early psychoanalytic experiment made possible the forms of collective action that later gave rise to patient administrative groups (PAGs) and a wider patient federation in the hospital. The second set concerns the place of PAGs in the wider organizational politics of the hospital. The struggle for representation provoked backlash. As wards challenged the authority of their custodians, their efforts were met with repression—not repression in the overt form of a Nurse Ratched, but with more subtle shifts in procedure and organization. Staff made strategic use of the traditional hallmarks of democratic governance—election, representation, deliberation, and constitution making—to contain and control wards.

Patients' organizations, described later, left numerous traces in the historical records of St. Elizabeths Hospital.[7] First, there are 428 cubic feet of administrative archives housed in Record Group 418 at the National Archives and Record Administration (NARA). This includes, for example, various annual reports of the administrative units of the hospital and sundry memoranda to and from the superintendent at the time, Winfred Overholser. Some ward dramas played out on a month-to-month timeline, requiring a careful look at the monthly reports of the various divisions and subunits in the hospital. Other files available at NARA were used to craft this case study, documents ranging from declassified reports on group therapy in the military to personal correspondence among high-level administrators.

Second, I've gathered works authored by various psychiatrists who worked in Howard Hall during this period. Articles published by Joseph Abrahams, Francis Tartaglino, and Bernard Cruvant were particularly helpful. Beyond published monographs in psychiatric journals like *Mental Hospitals* and the *American Journal of Psychiatry*, I had the good fortune to meet and conduct a series of interviews in 2014 with

Dr. Joseph Abrahams, ninety-eight years old at the time. When combined with a recently published 850-page, two-volume annotated collection of his session notes (originally typed up by patients), I was able to get a portrait of the early group intervention in Howard Hall at a unique level of granularity.

And finally, I've collected a variety of patient-authored works. The St. Elizabeths Health Science Library houses a major run of the *Howard Hall Journal* (later the *John Howard Journal*) and the *Elizabethan*, both patient-authored newspapers. The editorial pages of the *John Howard Journal* in particular were fruitful for mapping various patient attitudes.[8] As a condition of access to these files, I am not allowed to publish the names of the patient authors.[9]

In the following I offer an account of the rise, institutionalization, and demise of self-government in Howard Hall that, to the best of my ability, remains faithful to the available archival data. To paraphrase the words of a patient editor of the *Journal*: we're all swimmers in the depths of mental illness; as we dive into ourselves to fish for the meaning of our actions, let us remember not to indulge in telling tall "fish stories" about what we've found.[10]

THE PROBLEM OF COLLECTIVE ORGANIZATION

Howard Hall was the maximum security building of St. Elizabeths Hospital, tasked with caring for about 170 of the institution's most dangerous patients.[11] That group included men facing criminal charges found to be non compos mentis; those who had attacked other patients or staff; and in 1947, those admitted under the sex psychopath statute.[12] Official accounts paint a bleak picture of Howard Hall itself: "forbidding and cheerless," "very old," "obsolete equipment and furnishings," and a "medieval fortress."[13] Ezra Pound, perhaps St. Elizabeths most famous patient, used a more poetic adjective with a visiting confidant in 1946: "hell hole."[14]

Authoritarian control by a dedicated group of attendants made the difference between life and death on the nine wards of Howard Hall.[15] The reasons varied. One psychiatrist argued that a significant minority of the patients were "malcontents who, in their striving for power or as an expression of hostility, kept a good portion of the patient population in turmoil. The absence of a planned therapeutic program and the repressive atmosphere made excellent propaganda for their destructive efforts."[16]

One incident was particularly vivid in the minds of staff in the spring of 1946:

On March 6, 1946, Mr. Charles G. Repass, attendant on Howard Hall 1, was severely injured by [patient]. The patient stabbed the attendant in the glabella with a pointed piece of wooden molding. He was immediately given emergency attention. . . . In this regard I wish to point out the fact that there are a great many patients in the Howard Hall building with exceedingly assaultive tendencies. Very often the attendant, nursing, and physician personnel are subjected to great danger and not infrequently employees are injured in the performance of their regular duties.[17]

Howard Hall in the mid-1940s was, by all accounts, a unit feared by patients and staff alike.[18] After a particularly daring escape by two patients in April 1946, large floodlights were installed outside the walls to deter further attempts.[19] Bare and violent, the records from this period portray Howard Hall (in an irony to its namesake, the famous prison reformer John Howard) as a bastille, not as a therapeutic hospital.[20]

However, this time also marked a transition from St. Elizabeths as a "war-time hospital" to a "peace-time hospital": "The supply of foodstuffs, textiles, clothing, and other needed materials has increased substantially, although the costs have shown a disturbing increase. Personnel of all classes has become more plentiful, so that further attention to the treatment and other needs of the patients has been possible."[21] With that transition came a renewed spotlight on reform.

Psychiatric fashion, too, began to shift by the end of the decade. Psychoanalysis had come into its own during World War II. Talk therapy proved effective on the battlefield; as a consequence, it enjoyed a high status among professional psychiatrists in the 1940s and 1950s.[22] At a large institution like St. Elizabeths, one-on-one talk therapy wasn't feasible.[23] As an alternative, various psychoanalytically inspired group treatment methods were investigated and tested at the hospital. Superintendent Overholser, for example, sent staff to observe Jacob Moreno's "theater of psychodrama" program in New York in 1939, then implemented a version of the program at St. Es in the early 1940s.[24]

Drawing inspiration from Clifford Shaw, a sociologist at the University of Chicago, a newly hired psychoanalyst by the name of Joseph Abrahams became interested in the possibility of therapeutic intervention in Howard Hall.[25] The wards of Howard Hall at the time were segregated, and with the blessing of the hospital superintendent Abrahams began his group therapy experiment on the Black admission ward. While not stated explicitly in the records, it's clear that working with this population was a relatively low political risk for the hospital administration. There is a long, disturbing history of Black people being exploited in medicine and medical research at St. Es and beyond.[26] Moreover, those in Howard Hall, white or Black, were largely deemed lost causes.

Abrahams's notes describe the first day of the intervention:

> November 6, 1946. I began the session by "casually" sitting down on a bench at one end of the dayroom of the black admission ward. Two patients soon approached me, both in manacles.... I asked them how they were getting along. They responded with a request that I take their wristlets off. I suggested that we discuss that "problem" with the entire ward group. They said they didn't care how it was done. Those two patients then proceeded to assemble eight more patients, and we seated ourselves in a semicircle at the end of the dayroom. I explained that we were gathered to talk over problems on the ward, one of them being the wristlets on [the patient] and his partner, who appeared emotionally aroused. Three of the semicircle showed overt interest.[27]

In Abrahams's own account, in this first session he was "looking for the formation of the unity that marks a therapeutic community, a social unit separate from, but alongside the alienated world of the patients, and linked to the reality I was representing. I conceived that unity to be transactional in nature, if the definition of transaction is a unity of interacting entities. Moreover, ... that unity was a new reality, taking its place alongside accustomed reality."[28] In other words, the ambition of the initial intervention was not (nominally, at least) to jar patients into accepting a particular, external institutional reality; rather, it was to draw them into a consensus vision of reality defined by the interactions of members of that small group on the ward.

The goal of his psychoanalytic approach was to talk through the patients' inner disturbance, rather than to talk over it. Deliberation was at the heart of the theory. The patients' role in the "schizophrenic society" was, as much as possible, to help each other attain the insight and change needed to get along better in the group, then in the outside world.[29] Psychotics could come to recognize psychosis in others, even if they had difficulty recognizing it in themselves.

Twice a week Abrahams would come to Howard Hall. Not everyone present at the group spoke, so Abrahams would solicit participation in a loosely "representative" fashion: "Somebody would be here muttering, someone would be here masturbating, another would be lying around, you know, these were psychotic individuals. I would use the representative principle. Who was representing which factions of this group, and I would acknowledge that person."[30]

Abrahams would attempt to generate reactions ("by being evocative, sometimes provocative") from members of each faction in the group—to use some of the preceding language, the mutterers, the masturbators, the paranoid.[31] The group would also make representation and participation an explicit object of discussion, hashing out proper seating arrangements, who should chair the session, and the general goals of the group.[32] These discussions about group structure ranged from ordered to haphazard.[33]

During those first months of sessions, discussions could get heated, sometimes even leading to physical altercations: "The group became tense, and Bostic appeared agitated. He stood, and stated, in a determined, low voice, 'Vince, you're going to have to kill me.' Vince Jordan suddenly ripped off his coat and the two members met in the middle of the room and pummeled each other, mainly in the body. Members of the group, the attendant, and myself, attempted to separate the combatants. We succeeded, after several minutes of scuffling. Vince's nose was bloodied, and Bostic's lips lacerated on their inner aspects."[34]

Order, in the last resort, was maintained by "burly attendants" who would separate and isolate the offending parties. In most cases, however, conflict was managed by redirecting the agitated individual back to the group: "'Abrahams, you're a goddamn son-of-a-bitch.' 'Well, group, what do you think? Am I a goddamn son-of-a-bitch?' "Let's discuss that."[35] The goal of the group leader was to subtly conduct the group toward addressing a particular individual's problem behavior. The ultimate ambition was to provide a scaffolding for the group to conduct itself. In the most successful cases, the groups would be self maintaining, "with the sessions continuing after the doctor leaves, and at times when the doctor cannot appear under the general responsibility of the attendant."[36]

The dynamic of the group wasn't a simple function of its component parts. As individuals began to leave the Howard Hall for less restrictive wards (something rare in previous years), the inflow of new members didn't appear to disrupt the integrity of the group process. Reporting to his superiors in the hospital, Abrahams wrote, "While there is a constant flow of patients through the groups, the phenomena described seem to have sufficient momentum so as not to be seriously affected, although longer exposure per patient would be helpful."[37]

Higher-up members of the St. Elizabeths administration were uniformly positive about Abrahams's program.[38] In the margins of his first monthly report, for example, his supervisor, Bernard Cruvant, scribbled "Enthusiastic, interested, cooperative, and intelligent. A desirable man but needs tempering. Somewhat anxiety-ridden.—BAC [Bernard A. Cruvant]."[39] The perceived success of group psychotherapy in Howard Hall in those first few months facilitated its quick spread throughout the hospital.

The patients' responses to Abrahams's groups varied. Some toed the line: "Dr. Abrahams who works with us here in the Hall is someone to whom we are all very grateful for helping us solve our problems and finding out what brought us here. . . . Let us all pull together, and take our place in society together."[40] Others were less sure of the value of group therapy, "They [groups] are interesting, from the stand-point of applied therapeutics, but do they accomplish anything? . . . The main difficulty, as seen by Your Reporter, thus far, is that the Group seems to wander—they digress—and nothing seems to be done to correct this situation. Why?"[41] And some were more directly critical: "Yet I was hostile to group therapy at first. It seemed to me a cut-rate modification of individual psychotherapy, an ersatz, prostituted, watered down system evolved out of necessity, embellished with a new name, and a few flourishes of theory to make it appear respectable."[42]

Ward staff was another matter; nurses and attendants were more uniformly reticent to accept the changes.[43] Once quiet wards were now more lively; one began to hear the "more normal sounds" of conversation on the wards. Some of the attendants, moreover, feared that leniency would lead to difficulties in maintaining control and might even provoke rioting.[44] The facts that rioting did not happen, and that ward staff were either moved out of the hall or retrained in group psychotherapy, helped overcome, or at least contain, that friction.[45]

Once assembled as a group, the Black patients would use the session to discuss problems on the ward—privileges, visiting hours, food preparation—in addition to their psychiatric maladies.[46] One of the first patient requests was to the Red Cross for reading material and for opportunities for recreation. When these requests were granted, patients in the white wards took note and asked for group therapy in their section of Howard Hall.[47]

Where in early 1946 there were virtually no therapeutic activities, now, by early 1947, the hall became host to recreational therapy, occupational therapy, and psychodrama, along with a variety of others. Patients noticed the change. One, for example, commented that "many old time patients of Howard Hall are saying that the Hall is a much better place to live in than it was a few years ago. Many improvements have been noticed in the last year [1947] or so."[48]

Over the course of a year, group therapy expanded to include all the Black wards of Howard Hall (1946), then the white wards (June 1947), then to a larger integrated group (July 1947).[49] These integrated group sessions were held in the Howard Hall chapel, with as many as one hundred patients gathered at one time.

A key moment in the development of group therapy occurred during the summer of 1947. A significant, recurring complaint by patients in the Black therapy group concerned food in the hall—accusations that white patients were given greater portions, concerns about taste and quality of food, and worries about sanitation and preparation:

> Black Therapy Group Session #106. July 24, 1947. . . . Dr. Olinik had inves-tigated the food situation and I [Dr. Abrahams] transmitted to them that the food was divided on the basis of number of patients. This they obviously were not convinced of. Then there was much time spent, at least 25 minutes, on similar practical matters, such as the cleanliness of the inner courtyard and the poor performance of the barbers. I finally interrupted this by point-ing out again that I had no administrative standing or position in the running of Howard Hall. . . . I thought it would be better to bring these problems up with Dr. Cruvant or Dr. Olinick directly. The previous chair [of the therapy group] then claimed that the group had repeatedly asked Dr. Abrahams to bring Dr. Cruvant to one of these meeting but that so far Dr. Cruvant had not been present. I indicated that I would again remind Dr. Cruvant of the group's wish if I should see him.[50]

Dr. Cruvant, head of the Westside Service (the administrative unit containing Howard Hall), eventually agreed to meet with patients on the two admission wards. In these "administrative group" meetings, held every other week, the entire body of patients was allowed to voice its concerns.[51] Sessions were organized along New England "town meeting" lines, attended by the physician in charge, the supervisor of nurses, and attendants for the Howard Hall building. While tasked with remedying mundane issues on the ward, these sessions were still understood to be therapeutic. The hospital came to class these groups as "Administrative Therapy."[52] The "administrator as therapist," Cruvant writes in a pub-lished article from the period, "occupies a role roughly analogous to 'fac-ulty advisor' or 'sponsor' and is present only as a liaison representative to the hospital hierarchy."[53]

It was during Cruvant's sessions that the PAG was conceived, an organization of patients (described more thoroughly in the next sec-tion) in Howard Hall structured "along democratic lines of procedure, with officers and committees designed to function for the betterment of ward living conditions."[54] Like the sessions run by Abrahams, these psychotherapeutic groups were premised on the idea that patients could discuss other members' psychoses, even if they couldn't recognize their own individual psychosis. Administrative therapy built on this insight. In administrative groups patients constructed and engaged a consensus vision of the reality of ward problems. This meant, for example, that patients would rule out through discussion complaints thought to be nonreal (a nefarious plot by Mrs. Roosevelt, for instance) and create an agenda out of the remaining concerns.[55]

The role of the psychiatrist in group sessions was to prevent epistemic closure. The consensus reality of the group *included* the psychiatrist, who stood in for an outside vision of reality. The physician's presence in the group stood in for a reality that was authoritative but not definitive; his perspective was included in the deliberative process but didn't determine the outcome. In this vision of community, the ambition of guardianship was to ensure the translatability of group decisions to both the hospital (administrators, psychiatrists, other patients) and, in principle, the wider (sane) public. The ambition was to make both madness and wider hospital needs and interests mutually recognizable—to turn private claims into appreciably public ones.[56]

This kind of consensus building is a twist on the traditional image of able-minded dialogue partners that underpins most visions of collective deliberation. In Howard Hall, we have a vision of reason, of deliberation, without a traditional reasoner. Rationality (at least in theory) was an emergent property of patients working in concert, and deliberation was put in service of a shared, world-building project.

The first significant PAG action was the creation of a "food and welfare committee," composed of two members of each ward, to investigate and articulate the many complaints (noted previously) concerning the kinds of food being prepared in the hall's two dining rooms. Regular weekly meetings were held with Dr. Cruvant, the head cook, and a dietician. One patient, echoing Cruvant, wrote: "The most important achievement of the Food and Welfare Committee was that it brought to the attention of the hospital administrators, for the first time, the problems of the patients in an organized fashion that assured them they would be heard and given adherence. In turn, the patients were made aware of the many problems that the administration has to face in the selection and preparation of food, and each respected and made every effort to understand the position of the other."[57]

The successes of the food and welfare committee—successfully replacing "war-time boiled chicken with peace-time fried chicken" and institutionalizing audits of food quality, to name just two—encouraged the formation of other committees and shored up support for the PAG among patients.[58] The changes on the ward were a tremendous boost to patient morale, and patients "gained a sense of personal participation and a sense of responsibility for their own contributions to the welfare of the whole."[59]

Seeing the utility of the large, townhall–style administrative group, Cruvant decided to make ward attendance compulsory. Patients initially resisted this mandate: "It is sincerely believed that attendance would be greater, interest keener, and perception deeper, on the part of the Patients, were the Group Therapy Meetings to be attended on a voluntary basis, instead of a compulsory basis. By making attendance Compulsory, a wall of prejudice has been built; which, we believe, would immediately crumble if the Compulsory 'status' were removed."[60] Eventually, however, patients complied with the new expectations.[61] In addition, patients were also restricted from talking about institutional privileges like parole and discharge in their regular group therapy sessions.[62] Psychiatrists claimed that administrative concerns interfered with group psychotherapy, and that administrative therapy was better suited to sifting out the "reality" of patients' particular complaints.

Over the next ten years group work, including administrative groups like the PAG in Howard Hall, spread throughout the entire hospital.[63] Democracy became good therapy.

PATIENT ADMINISTRATIVE GROUPS (PAGS)

But what did self-government look like? First, consider the formal structure of the PAG in Howard Hall. Before the demolition of the original Howard Hall building (and the move to the newly constructed John Howard Pavilion), the whole patient population of the hall would nominate, then elect, officers to conduct its sessions. Nominations and elections were conducted by a show of hands or a voice vote.[64] The PAG would meet semimonthly; the first meeting was to hammer out an agenda and the second to conduct a session in accordance with that agenda. The vast majority of patients were present, filling the Howard Hall chapel to capacity.[65] The patients would periodically draw up new bylaws for the PAG, which had to be approved by the administrative authorities.[66] The chief of service, or one of his representatives, was always present at these meetings. In 1959, when the patients were moved to the John Howard Pavilion, the structure was modified. Under the new system, each of the twelve wards had its own PAG, which operated as a unit for that ward. The members of each PAG would elect three members to serve on a patients' administrative council (PAC) that would represent the entire hall: a chair, a vice-chair, and a secretary. Leading the PAC was an elected executive committee, consisting of three patients.[67] Each ward chairman would have a copy of the bylaws of the council.[68] As in the previous system, two meetings were held each month, an agenda meeting and a business meeting.

The representative structure of the PAG and PAC created tensions. In a "Dear Abby" type column in the *John Howard Journal* titled "Cousin Mot," one patient penned the following: "Dear Cousin: I am the Vice-Chairman on my ward. Between the Chairman and the Secretary I never get a word in edgewise, my voice is never heard. What can I do?—Name and ward withheld on request."[69] In another column, an anonymous patient questioned the possibility of finding a chairman of "such standards" that can "distinguish con-gaming from sincerity" and can judge "the sick from the patients who are just trying to beat their charges"; after all, "if any *sincere* committed patient had peace of mind why in hell would he be here in the first place?"[70] Rephrased, representation only makes sense if the representative is cool, collected, and rational—a stark contrast, one might assume, to the mean John Howard patient. This catch-22 haunted not only PAGs, but also, as we'll see, leadership in the larger patient federation.

In addition to PAG (and PAC) officers, patients would be nominated to particular committees. Committees ran the gamut of ward functions: food committee, recreation committee, dance committee, occupational therapy committee, and a school committee, among a host of others. Some committees were standing (education), while others were specific to particular events (dance). The various committees forwarded multiple purposes. On the one hand, they provided a vehicle to organize ward life in the absence of explicit administrative programming. The education committee, for example, organized classes for patients in the absence of an educational program in the hall.[71] "Courses are included from very elementary ones to more advanced courses, such as French and Accounting. The instructors are all patients, and the program is under the general supervision of one of the patients who has a Master's degree in education from the University of Rochester, but who unfortunately became involved in some sexual difficulties. The program is now functioning very smoothly, considering its recent installation."[72]

On the other hand, some committees, like the social and recreational committee, were tasked with generating patient enthusiasm for hall events—from patient productions like "Schitzofrolics" to more mundane events like interhall dances.[73] And still more committees were tasked with vetting proposals for policy changes with the administration.[74]

The medium became the message. Adherence to rules and procedures became significant in itself. When patient representatives were thought to have overstepped their authority, they were reprimanded by the patient population.[75] Likewise, when members of the PAC made promises to the administration it wasn't authorized to make or couldn't keep, they faced rebuke from hospital staff.[76]

While the strength of PAGs varied by ward, the central currency in all PAG negotiations with the hospital administration was privileges.[77] Privileges to use the courtyard. Privileges to have coed dances. Conditions for transfer to more privileged wards. Officials in the PAGs and PAC were tasked with both obtaining privileges for the unit and securing those privileges once obtained.[78] Every privilege gained was paired with a concomitant responsibility. One physician offers the following example: "The first dance, attended by female hospital patients, was held in Howard Hall. It was extremely enjoyable to all concerned apparently and there were no untoward incidents. . . . I believe the patients are so jealous of this added privilege that they, themselves, will be very careful to avoid any untoward incidents."[79]

When problems did arise, the administration could hold the PAC, not simply individual patients, accountable: "During one of the dances in the gymnasium a door was forced, resulting in clandestine contacts between some of the patients on our service and some of the female patients who were attending the dance. As a result of this it was necessary to suspend a number of recreational activities and review the entire situation with personnel, patients, and, specifically, with the P.A.C., which, as a self-government group, was charged with and accepted some share of the responsibility for this sort of behavior. Proper and appropriate safeguards and steps toward self-government will need to be taken."[80]

Leverage, however, was not just on the side of the hospital administration. For one, with a chronic shortage of employees, the PAG often took over responsibility for functions previously in the ambit of ward personnel.[81] These functions ranged from operating elevators to chaperoning recreational activities.[82] In addition, the PAG produced a variety of efficiencies for an overburdened, understaffed administration.[83] Most significantly, it outsourced monitoring of ward conditions (supervision of ward staff, cleanliness, food quality) to the patients themselves; quality communication between the administration functioned as a form of cheap, decentralized monitoring. Furthermore, the PAG provided a release valve for ward complaints that would otherwise be time consuming to address or adjudicate.[84]

Self-government and the PAG were as much cultures as formal structures. Even proposals for new therapeutic programs had to be couched in the language of democracy and civic voluntarism. In reviewing a proposal for a family dinner program, the first assistant physician of the hospital wrote:

> Mrs. Bushart mentions the family dinner program in the Red Cross Building on Tuesday evenings and since Mrs. Harris and I have attended this I have thought a great deal about how it could be utilized, perhaps on a modified scale on each of the Services. There is an almost uncanny home style atmosphere that would provide I think, a very tantalizing taste of what one is missing in here no matter how good the food is. Since such a small group would have to be undemocratic however, it would have to start with the patient government on the Service and not in a highly planned fashion.[85]

The understood civic and therapeutic function of self-government was to prepare patients for life outside the hospital. Some patients, however, could never reasonably expect to live on their own on the outside. The best these patients could hope for, according to psychiatrists, was to become a useful "hospital citizen."[86] A similar belief was shared among patients; one dark and humorous patient poem, for instance, suggests that even in death one is just moving to another asylum ward ("And when I saw Peter at the pearly gates, I asked, 'Where's the attendant up here?!'").

The existence of the category of "hospital citizen" suggests an important dis-analogy between the civic education of asylum patients and the civic education of youth. The civic curriculum of the hospital accepted the possibility, even the likelihood, that many individuals *by their nature* could not and should not (that is, it's therapeutically inappropriate to) strive for full civic freedom. Some, importantly, argued that the loss of social skills, concern for the outside world, and so on among a subset of patients was actually the result, not the cause, of long-term residence in a mental hospital.

To that wrinkle in the civic curriculum, it's important to add another. Hospital psychiatrists held an image of democracy *as* treatment and not, importantly, democracy *in* treatment. The result is that the ambition to "detotalize" ward culture had the aim of mirroring voluntary confinement, not engaging in a kind of democratic constitution making. Patients, however, played on the ambiguity between *as* and *in*— collectively organizing concerns, pushing the administration, and using the language of democracy and legitimacy to pressure the hospital to respond to their concerns.

While the language and culture of self-government became dominant, patients actively deliberated over the substantive meaning of the hospital's vision of civic education. A flare-up in the *John Howard Journal* during the twilight of self-government at St. Es is illustrative. In an editorial that would cause outrage on the wards, the patient editor of the *Journal* wrote:

> Last things first, the doctors, if they treat us like mischievous children, are not without reasons in doing so. Most of us are here as a result of a variety of criminal offenses and are, therefore, rebels—in rebellion against just about every form of authority and the lawful ethics of society. Furthermore, we are, basically, an irresponsible group of passive-aggressive individuals who think that father (the doctor) and mother (the nurse) should cater to our every whim; and, when he or she doesn't, we do everything contrary to make things as difficult for them as possible (or so we think) and, in most instances, in making things difficult for them, we thus make things more difficult for ourselves.[87]

The demand for changes on the ward such as increased psychiatric attention and more privileges is less an example of self-government and more like children throwing a tantrum in front of their parents.

In response, a patient wrote a tract that is worth excerpting at some length:

> John Howard—Pavilion??—is partitioned into four, non-communicating levels of three wards each; comprising a total of twelve separate—confined groups—contained—placid—docile ... constrained, by the very nature of their controlled divisionment, to impotent competition for unimportant totems of recognition. Twelve groups, rendered manageable by of the oldest approved tactics known to autocratic governments: The diminishing appeasement of group representation.... Over 4,000 years ago, twelve separate tribes cohered, unified and, as one body, moved ... We are twelve separate wards; and, at once, we are 300 separate individuals, as isolated from one another in purpose and co-operation as the twelve wards are from their neighbor.... How can the conditions in John Howard be changed? ... Behold, the people are one ... And they have all one language; ... And now, nothing will be restrained from them which they have imagined to do ...

And it shall come to pass, that when all the people shout . . . The wall shall fall flat.[88]

Self-government, in this account, is an appeasement tactic fit for an authoritarian regime. Only when the patients are genuinely united, when they speak in one language, can the walls of the asylum that divide and confine them "fall flat."[89] Browsing the pages of the *Journal* more widely, one gets the impression that no amount of scrutiny seemed to make the confusion around the meaning of self-government evaporate; no amount of heated debate appeared to boil it off.

On the whole, the scope of PAGs touched almost all facets of ward life, from therapy, to administration, to patient culture. The PAG was integrated into a variety of therapeutic activities on the wards, so much so that the historical record is littered with comments referring to patient government as a "dynamic force in the rehabilitation and reorientation of these patients and serves as a basis for the entire therapeutic program."[90]

THE PATIENT FEDERATION

Administrative therapy, as noted previously, spread throughout the hospital over the course of the 1950s. During the mid-1950s, physicians in the Dorothea Dix Service organized a series of self-government groups modeled on those pioneered in Howard Hall.[91] The accounts of the "spontaneous" emergence of administrative groups that litter the records of St. Es follow a basic template, and the psychiatric narrative in Dix was no exception. An apathetic ward, through the medium of group therapy and ward self-government, was transformed into an active patient community.[92]

The administrative groups, like those in Howard Hall, began to grow—electing officials, creating committees, and negotiating proposals with the administration.[93] Eventually referring to themselves as a "patients' congress," patients began to take on more responsibilities on the wards. While some of these responsibilities were related to entertainment or general programming, others had larger administrative consequences.[94] Organized patient labor, for example, eased the pressure created by staff shortages.[95] One staff member quipped, "We have used patient volunteer help at all levels in the [hospital] Branch, and, short of being provided with keys to the hospital, a number of these patients have provided assistance almost at the level of full-time employees."[96] Again, the psychiatric justification for self-government was used to overcome the initial resistance of ward staff (nurses, attendants) to expansions of patient privileges and ward responsibilities. Staff either mouthed the institutional line or were transferred to another ward.[97]

The inertia of the patients' congress was toward accepting more responsibility for ward administration. The head of service writes: "I was most gratified by the decorum, intelligence, and serious interest that they showed toward a number of factors beyond simple entertainment for the service. I am happy to report that the congress itself is growing somewhat restless in the limitations of its duties and is now drawing up a constitution by which it offers itself as an intelligent organization for our use in matters of communication, service sociology, and even discipline. I visualize, not too clearly as yet, a very progressive usefulness of the congress for the service as well as the patients."[98]

Many of these responsibilities were traditionally tasks of ward staff. Among the more routine, for example, was the working out of housekeeping regulations and the monitoring of their enforcement. Others were nonroutine: the patients' congress "worked out the doubling up of wards, freeing certain ward personnel for these [staff] conferences."[99] Administrators noticed these advantages and readily ceded more ground to the group.[100]

Patients themselves saw the congress as a vehicle to voice disapproval with new administrative policies: a recent order concerning the racial segregation of dancing was placed before the patients' congress, who decided that the best way to handle the matter was to stop dancing altogether.[101] Like psychiatrists and hospital administrators, savvy patients understood the group as a potential vehicle of expression and action.

In the spring of 1957, the patients' congress put together a proposal for a hospital-wide patient federation.[102] As envisioned by a former patient, the new group would be a tool for communication among patients and a means to collectively bargain with the hospital administration.[103] The first meeting of the patient federation was on April 2, and hospital administrators were generally enthusiastic about its potential.[104] The director of special services served as a liaison between the patients and the administrative staff: "The representatives from the services are taking this very seriously with the understanding that hospital rules must be observed."[105] Once Superintendent Overholser explicitly approved the federation, patients from all of the divisions of the hospital (including the Westside Service that housed the John Howard Pavilion) were represented.[106]

The original vision of the patient federation was as a vehicle to organize all of the patient groups in the hospital into a single bargaining unit.

Individual wards would deliberate, then send delegates to an executive hall council. The executive council, in turn, would send delegates to the hospital-wide federation.[107] The structure they built was anticipatory, a vision of a kind of institutional democracy to come. More active wards (such as Dix, where the idea for the federation began in the first place) would sustain the federation as other divisions of the hospital worked on building collective capacity in their wards.[108]

Though a few members of the staff opposed these developments, the majority saw the federation as an opportunity to cultivate the habits of citizenship necessary for patients to return to society. The publication and subsequent prominence of Maxwell Jones's *The Therapeutic Community* only added to this intuition. Again, democracy was good medicine; it "discharged negative tensions through planning" and can do "as much for [patients] as do most citizens' associations in the community."[109] More modestly, the goal was to approximate the conditions of *voluntary* confinement.[110] The purpose of the patient federation was to "provide a forum for discussion by the patients of hospital matters, living conditions, administration and recreation, permitting the exchange of ideas [and] growth of patient civic participation as well as [providing] a source to the hospital of suggestions and recommendations."[111] A reference to the patient federation even made an appearance in the annual reports of the hospital.[112]

Within a year, however, the patient federation began to ruffle both psychiatric staff and administrators. As patients started to challenge the authority of their custodians, the hospital, in various ways, pushed back. Repeated demands for improvement of hospital conditions left some administrators exasperated: the federation's "chief concern seems to be their own personal comfort in the hospital rather than any constructive plans for life outside of the hospital" and created administrative "complications."[113] Three complications, in particular, are salient in the hospital archives.

First, patient voice created demands on staff time and attention. Meeting minutes and patient-authored "letters of suggestion" had to be reviewed, sessions had to be directed (or, at a minimum, loosely supervised), and hospital regulations had to be standardized. This was compounded by a perceived lack of effectiveness. From the perspective of administrative staff, one of the central virtues of patient government (at whatever level in the hospital) was its ability to mobilize patient interest in hospital affairs, particularly hospital events. Lackluster performance in generating turnout for a talent show and a series of hospital-sponsored expert panels further undermined the group's utility in the minds of staff.[114]

Second, the democratic mandate of the group was ambiguous. As noted previously, the hope was that organizational innovation, mobilization, and representation would be connected in a virtuous cycle. In a sentence: it was an organizational anticipation of democratic participation.[115] However, "Somehow, the delegates are not representative of the groups back in the services, and only in rare instances do the delegates come to the meeting with directives from the service group to bring up matters of general interest or replies to questions posed for consideration by the Federation. Except for W. A. White [Service] and Dix [Service], who do manage to elect patients alert and interested in patient organization, the "delegates" are largely passive, easily swayed by the best talkers in the group."[116]

Without representativeness, the patient federation was no different than any other ward council. Staff claimed that it was a "federation" in name only. At best, the concerns expressed by patients were the product of distorted participation, a kind of populist excess. The federation's pretense of democratic authorization, of representativeness, obscured its only real function: as a group therapy session for participating members. And it is precisely this argument that was eventually used to divert resources away from the patient federation.

The third, and most damning, complication concerned the institutional location of the federation. Part of the complication over location was literal, about where to physically house the federation.[117] But the heart of the issue was its location among the various systems of knowledge in the hospital. Ambiguity over jurisdiction facilitated the dismantling of the federation. From the beginning, staff in the Special Services Branch (which housed the patient federation) called into question the scope of the federation's authority: "some discussion by the staff on just what are matters proper to patient discussion in meetings such as these; at present there are no limits delineated, making it difficult to advise the group. The [staff] advisor questions the advisability of making official memorandum paper available to patient government groups for purposes of writing memos to staff requesting actions from staff on matters that staff is best able to judge."[118]

Eventually the recreation department in Special Services made the case (as noted earlier) that delegates were not representative, nor did delegates forward the goal of increasing interest in the hospital's patient programs. They made the case that the group was *psychiatric*, simply another group therapy session, and that a physician ought to be the one to direct the group. However, psychiatrists were ambivalent (at best) about the therapeutic value of the federation *as* group therapy: "It seems that after relatively short periods of hospitalization the patients tend to socialize with the motivation for making this a 'happy home' rather than for reentering a competitive outside activity. This suggests that our permissive ego supportive approach while effective with the psychotic and even distressed neurotic patients nevertheless may not be too desirable and is not stimulative to the patients who have attained good reality testing in this environment."[119] The psychiatric arguments that had previously justified PAGs, administrative therapy, and the patient federation, while not being rejected, were now being minimized, distinguished, and contained.

Crucially, at this time St. Es began to witness the transformative impact of tranquilizing drugs like Thorazine and Serpasil. What was truly transformational about these drugs, however, was not the medication itself but the conviction that it was possible to *prescribe* solutions to both ward problems and mental illness more generally.[120]

A report on in-house clinical trial of these new drugs from November 9, 1954, is effusive:

> The efficacy of these two drugs is demonstrated, among other ways, by the drive on the part of some of the physicians and ward personnel to obtain additional supplies of the drug for additional patients. In order to be able better to evaluate the results of these drugs, we have restricted their use to limited areas where arrangements have been made for appropriate recording of results. In one instance, I am told, the nurses offered to purchase, themselves, additional supplies of Serpasil because of the promising results obtained previously with one or two of the patients.[121]

By 1958, just after the creation of the hospital-wide federation, the balance of treatment efforts had shifted to drugs. One physician lamented, "During the past year there have been no innovations in either the care or treatment of the patients. Tranquilizing drugs have been used in enormous quantities which have certainly controlled disturbed conduct, permitted opening of many of the wards and extended privileges to an ever increasing number of patients."[122] Tranquilizing drugs offered a means to maintain order and, under certain conditions, to give patients greater control over the management of their own psychotic symptoms.

Under pressure, the therapeutic justification that propped up the federation collapsed. By August 1959 the authority of the patient congress in Dix was gutted, and the patient federation was disbanded.[123]

MAD DEMOCRACY

"We are 300 divided individuals. A shotgun loaded with bird-shot against a mastodon."[124] In broad strokes, the preceding account details the institutional mechanisms that made it possible, made it reasonable, to include the mad in ward governance at St. Es in the middle of the century. The informal, patient-driven innovations that emerged out of Abrahams's original group therapy intervention were institutionalized by the hospital administration. Bolstered by administrative needs (staff shortages, efficiency), intellectual fashion (the rise of psychoanalysis), and psychiatric authorization (deliberation as reality testing), patient self-government groups thrived. The unruly and the unmanageable, the mad, became newly governable.[125] Patient speech and action became legible not only to various professions within the hospital, but also to fellow patients.

Admittedly these institutional developments add up to an odd image, perhaps a mad image, of democratic politics. Many will be uncomfortable with the characterization of the organizational politics of St. Elizabeths as *democratic*. Potemkin, maybe. But democratic? For social theorists like Goffman, where we began this chapter, patient self-government was at best an unsatisfying answer to fears of autocracy. At worst, it papered over political questions entirely. Whether one focuses on the original group therapy sessions in Howard Hall or the strategic use of devices like elections, constitution making, and deliberation in the more formalized PAGs, it would be a mistake to describe hospital wards, without qualification, as democratically organized.[126]

A through line connecting St. Es to wider trends in care in the 1960s and 1970s is that those who embraced "community" approaches to mental health tended to sidestep more fundamental questions of power at the base of ward-custodian relationship. Judi Chamberlin, former patient and cofounder of the Mental Patients Liberation Front, notes, "The method of the therapeutic community is described as democratic, but only if one accepts the strange definition of democracy [by psychiatrists] as a situation in which 'one person was responsible but he permitted the group decision to prevail with the understanding that he could overrule it if he wished.'"[127] This is as true of adherents to Maxwell Jones's therapeutic community as it is of more controversial experiments like R. D. Laing's Kingsley Hall.[128] The glamorization of "community" ignores a glaring contradiction: "the unacknowledged separations and distinctions between those who came as healers and those who came to be healed."[129]

However, in democratic politics there is not, as in every jigsaw puzzle, only one picture into which all the pieces fit. The story of patients at St. Elizabeths is as much a case study of the plasticity of power and ideology as it is of innovation and democratic imagination. Glossing the institutional features of patient self-government as simple instruments of authoritarianism, or mere ideology, misses the heart of the politics of ward government.

Stories of institutional creation, transformation, or decay tend to emphasize one of two sources of change: top-down or bottom-up. The typical top-down tale starts with elites, whether social movement leaders or elected officials, and seeks to demonstrate how institutions are determined by the laws, policies, or practices forwarded by those elites. Those emphasizing the bottom-up view portray institutions as emerging spontaneously from the norms, customs, beliefs, and values of individuals within a society, with written law and policy only formalizing what is mainly shaped by the attitudes and actions of individuals. Both positions, of course, are caricatures—and most actually existing views fall somewhere between these two extremes. What's often set to the side is not one source of change or the other, but their larger symmetry.[130]

As I understand it, the politics of patient self-government at St. Elizabeths was caught up in a strange kind of feedback loop. Democracy *as* therapy met democracy *in* therapy. There was a generative relationship between the institutional processing of patient claims for voice and the democratic processing of the hospital itself.[131] By the former, I mean the molding of patient participation to secure and extend the authority of those already in power. By the latter, I mean both patients' recourse to group participation as a way to navigate their precarious existence and the unsettling of foundational questions about who ought to govern asylum life. While interest groups can shape policy, it's also true that policies can form new interest groups.[132] Democracy as therapy did more than simply alter the incentive structure for participation; it also, as we've seen, shaped the identities, goals, and collective efficacy of wards.

After early experiments in democratic participation at St. Elizabeths and, later, the Yale Psychiatric Institute, "therapeutic communities" in the United States ultimately developed the hierarchical form they take today.[133] For mad citizens inside and outside of custodial care, fear of violence, social stigma, fragmented interests, coordination problems, co-optation, and a lack of community-level institutional support all persist. Democratic citizenship and psychiatric provision continue, unproductively, to be set against each other. And mass confinement of the mad in the prison system makes the conversation more pressing.[134]

However, at each step patients have pushed back. The core of mad activism has been the pursuit of a resolution, or dissolution, of this tension between democracy and care.[135] Benjamin Reiss argues that the legacy of the moral treatments of the nineteenth-century asylum—attending lectures, writing for institutional newspapers, participating in theatrical productions—still lingers in more modern concerns for civic education through "therapeutic community" and "patient-government structures."[136] At the heart of the legacy of moral treatment, he suggests, is a contradiction that contains the seeds of its own undoing. To insist that controlling a patient's environment could cure mental illness ultimately begs the question of who is doing the controlling, and on what terms.[137] For activists like Judi Chamberlin, and the wider consumer, survivor, ex-patient movement (C/S/X) in the United States, a true alternative is one in which basic decision-making power is in the hands of those the facility exists to serve.

CHAPTER 4

Community Control in Custody

In the early 1970s long-standing practices of custodial rule faced a general crisis of legitimacy. Hundreds of rebellions roiled the US prison system between 1971 and 1973 alone.[1] During this period of turmoil, a number of wardens responded by seeking the consent of the governed.[2] They doubled-down on organizational techniques like prisoner councils, collective bargaining, grievance committees, and even constitution making to calm the tempest. Some explicitly invoked language from earlier efforts in the War on Poverty (1964–) to justify their actions, calling for the "maximum feasible participation" of prisoners.[3] In doing so, they sparked a lesser-known public debate over what role, if any, prisoners should play in the operation of prisons and jails.

For some, the push for community control resonated with republican visions of democracy. That is, there was an emphasis on localism, a vibrant civil society, and active individual participation. Prisons, no less than town halls, are potential sites of civic renewal. Others were more reticent. For them, the conceptual stretching of "community control" from the War on Poverty to community control *in custody* created a category error. Organizational devices like prisoner councils (which I detail later) are more appropriately classed with various other techniques employed by twentieth-century totalitarian regimes, like those the *judenrat* used to govern the ghetto and the *sovety aktiva* used in the gulag.[4]

Even if adherents of community control are too sanguine in their praise of ward participation, critics are too quick to dismiss democratization

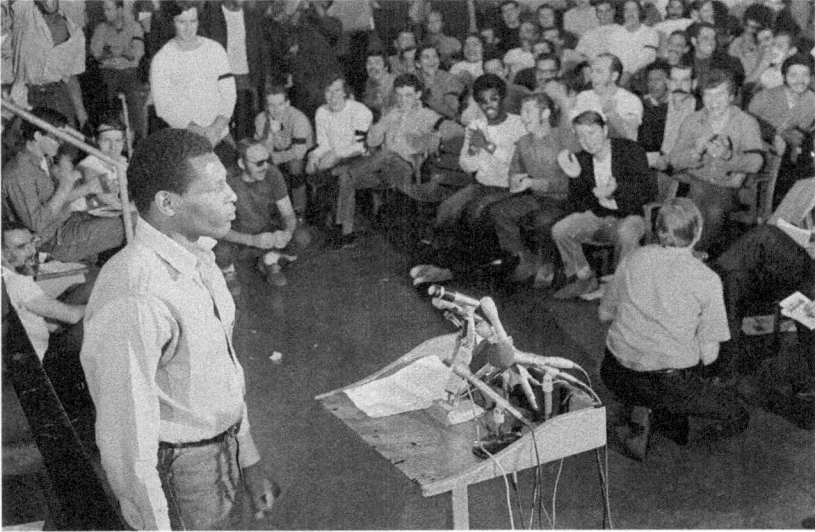

FIGURE 4. A prisoner at Massachusetts Correctional Institution at Walpole speaking at a rally for better conditions after the Attica rebellion, September 29, 1971. *Source:* Brearley Collection, Boston Public Library.

efforts. Or so I try to establish here. I suggest that the central weakness of the community control tradition is not this or that organizational design choice, but rather reformers' tendency to locate both problems, and the solutions to those problems, only in wards themselves. Rather than offer an alternative to the exclusion thesis, advocates of community control in custody largely reaffirmed the same worldview.

Unlike the previous chapter, on St. Elizabeths Hospital, or the next, on the Walpole prison rebellion, this chapter is not rooted in a particular archive. If those two chapters are the central pillars of this book, the analysis that follows in this chapter is the supportive cabling joining them. To present a sketch of the basic features of community control in custody, I draw heavily from the work of reform-minded prison wardens, particularly J. E. Baker and Tom Murton, outsider activists like John Irwin and Angela Davis, and a number of more recent scholarly works on ward self-government.[5] The implicit perspective of the pages that follow is one of would-be system designers: administrators, wardens, government officials, intellectuals, and social movement leaders. In occupying that perspective, my aim is to make sense of the self-description, and self-understanding, of community control by various elites. I want to understand how a certain political theory was held at a certain time and place and to examine what interventions and techniques made that conception of custody not only possible but plausible.

The scattered conversation about ward participation flamed out almost as quickly as it caught fire. However, revisiting this intellectual moment is not simply of antiquarian interest. Though one of its boldest iterations, it isn't the only iteration of community control.[6] Community control in custody is a part of our collective unconscious that hasn't been reckoned with; it has been repressed but not eliminated from discussions of prison and hospital reform. Bringing the features of this tradition to the conscious mind can give us purchase on a recurring set of empirical questions and normative intuitions that continue to influence efforts to reform, transform, or even abolish custody.

THE PRISON COMMUNITY

Before describing particular institutional design schemes, I offer a few words on the philosophy of community control that came to prominence during the War on Poverty and that prison reformers, in turn, tried to remix.

The Community Action Program (CAP) attempted to reform state bureaucracy in a way that married welfare provision with local control. Instead of directing resources toward anti-poverty programs directly, CAP created institutions for communities to control how those resources, delivered in the form of block grants, were distributed. At the highest level of generality, community control was the demand by groups that have traditionally held little power for enhanced roles in the shaping of policies that vitally affect their interests.[7]

The larger debate over community control during the late 1960s wrestled with at least two competing images of political order. On the one hand, left-leaning reformers invoked the long-standing tradition of participatory democracy. Like the urban rebellions during the late 1960s, the uprisings in prisons during the early 1970s were seen as demands not only for improved conditions but for voice. This intellectual lineage runs from Lloyd Ohlin, Richard Cloward, and Francis Piven to George Jackson and the wider movement for Black Power. On the other hand, from the right reformers drew from a liberal law and order legacy, from Daniel Moynihan and Edward Banfield to James Q. Wilson and John DiIulio. As expressed in Moynihan's famous tract on the War on Poverty, for this group of thinkers "maximum feasible participation" was maximum feasible *misunderstanding*, a recipe for resentment, mismanagement, and general lawlessness. Thinkers in the latter tradition ultimately came to define both prison and wider welfare policy.[8]

While there is no one shared account of community control, all embraced two features. First, the relevant unit of analysis was "the community"; reformers had in mind the scale of a small town or a city neighborhood. The general view among proponents of community control was that "people should have a chance to experience self-government in communities as small as several hundred or several thousand people wherever possible."[9] Second, advocates embraced the principle of decentralization, the idea that public decision-making ought to be devolved to the lowest feasible level.[10] In the context of prison reform, the push for community control was not simply local control *over* prisons, but *in* prisons. And the same two central ordering principles applied: a focus on the community as a political unit and decentralized (or devolved) government.

The analogy between prison and community isn't as far-fetched as it might seem at first glance. In Donald Clemmer's *The Prison Community*, for instance, the prison is "both an area of service and an area of participation." He notes that the history of any given prison is the chronicle of a community where thousands of people live out segments of their lives—not only prisoners and staff but those connected to them.[11] To be sure, the analogy has limits. The difference between a town of five thousand people and a penitentiary housing the same number makes this clear. Discrepancies aside, a long line of reformers have understood the prison as a self-contained social system.

The second feature of community control, devolved government, took the form of a call for "detotalization" and "democratization." The former term, *pace* Erving Goffman, refers to the transformation of a rigidly coercive system into an institutional culture characterized by pluralism and political consciousness. We saw a similar idea at work at St. E's when reformers aimed, as much as possible, to approximate an open ward at Howard Hall (that is, *voluntary* confinement). The latter term, democratization, denotes a process whereby prisoners are transformed from mere subjects of rule to competent citizens.[12]

Mutatis mutandis, those two features influenced a number of design choices in US prisons during this period. To be clear, full implementation of community control principles in prisons would have been nothing short of a bureaucratic revolution. The three design choices described here are at best echoes of a common ideology. Unlike its counterpart on the outside, custodial community control never had a clear mouthpiece. Nevertheless, its central principles can be reconstructed from the organizational practices embraced by prison administrators during this time.

Multilevel Grievance Procedures

During the 1960s and 1970s, increased attention was given to complaint procedures within prisons. Complaint procedures are an administrative, as opposed to legislative or judicial, means through which prisoners can express and resolve their grievances.[13] Complaints ran the gamut of mistreatments, ranging from officer abuse to the denial of medical needs. Since the 1970s these procedures have been the primary avenue by which prisoners name, blame, and make claims about problems in prison.[14]

Grievance procedures came in various colors. Warden Baker described three core types: ombudsman, grievance commissions, and multilevel appeals procedures. The first two emphasized independent powers of investigation. Variants of the latter form, however, sometimes included prisoner participants. "Multi-level grievance procedures," Baker writes, "involve the submission of complaints to a designated individual within an institution, with provision for appeals to successively higher levels within the organization and, in some instances, to a person or group outside the corrections agency."[15] Over half of states with these procedures permitted hearings on particular complaints. And nearly a third of the procedures with hearings gave prisoners, together with staff, a decision-making role.[16]

In Louisiana, for instance, a prisoner grievance committee was established in 1973 that provided for

> a General Assembly consisting of members elected by the residents of each housing unit and by each bona fide organization within the institution had been in operation not less than six months, to serve a one-year term with indefinite succession possible. The Assembly in turn elects from its membership an Executive Committee of seven, who may serve no more than two consecutive terms, to be generally representative of the various areas and facilities of the institution. The purpose of the committee is to receive and categorize prisoner complaints for presentation to an Administration Committee whose members include the warden, deputy warden, assistant wardens for custody and treatment, and the business manager. An employee, mutually acceptable to both committees, acts as a liaison between the groups.[17]

The Executive Committee recorded the results of its investigation of a complaint. Together with statements by supporting witnesses and any related documents, this information was then presented to the General Assembly for discussion and recommendation. In accordance with the recommendation, the Executive Committee then would negotiate with the Administration Committee for a mutually acceptable resolution.

The general rationale for prisoner participation in the grievance process was twofold: "to place the greatest amount of decision-making authority on the persons who must live with the results of the decisions, and to provide a forum for accommodation between opposing points of view."[18]

Prisoner Councils

Grievance procedures have a relatively recent history. While prisoner councils came to have increasing prominence during the late 1960s, their roots are much older. For at least a half century prior to that councils had been the primary organizational device for communicating prisoners' points of view to administrators.[19]

Prisoner councils (and unions, described later) provided prisoners with a formal vehicle through which their collective needs and concerns could be identified, discussed, and communicated to the administration of the institution. They were formally recognized associations, comprised of elected representatives of the prisoner population who were tasked with regularly bringing concerns on behalf of that population to the prison authorities. In practice, of course, councils varied in "structure, function, and power, but most operate[d] as a representative body with a formal constitution and an executive leadership that consult[ed] inmates on a wide range of issues, deliberates, and communicate[d] the needs of prison inmates vis-a-vis the institution, meeting regularly with staff and prison managers."[20]

Unlike multilevel grievance procedures, most prisoner councils did not consider individual complaints during meetings. As a result, this approach excluded a substantial portion of grievances from the jurisdiction of councils. According to Warden Baker, the view was that their inclusion would obstruct a principal goal: the advocacy of new or changed institutional policy.[21]

The degree of prisoner involvement varied. Some councils, like the one at Charlestown penitentiary discussed in greater depth later in this chapter, were simply advisory. Others, however, provided wider opportunities for prisoner participation. The Resident Government Council (RGC) at the penitentiary in Walla Walla, Washington, was one of the most expansive. A former RGC officer reflected on his feelings about the early years of the council: "The RGC had distinctive voting rights and privileges, we could call Olympia [the state capital], we could set up our own press conferences. We could call in reporters when we wanted to. We could take pictures, we could, you know, write out what we wanted to write out, we could send out, we could write out our own newspaper. We had all those discretionary situations that the former [advisory] councils never had. We even made decisions on the budget for awhile."[22]

Prisoner councils existed in more than half of adult prisons in 1973. By 1980 the use of councils had declined to less than one jurisdiction in three.[23]

Prison Unions

A call for a nationwide prisoner union emerged in the early 1970s. Donald Tibbs dates the ending of the Folsom prison strike on November 23, 1970, as the official start of the prisoner union movement in the United States. One of the demands in the manifesto of the striking prisoners at Folsom, demand 12, was "that inmates be allowed to form or join labor unions."[24] In the months immediately following the strike, outside activists in California formed the United Prisoner Union. Unions, advocates argued, provided an alternative method to riots and disturbances to pressure prison administrators.[25] Within two years, prisoner unions had spread across the country, from California to Michigan, New York, Massachusetts, and Rhode Island.

Consider the North Carolina Prisoners' Labor Union (NCPLU), which would become the subject of a major Supreme Court decision at the end of the decade: "[Prisoner] Brooks went to considerable lengths to legitimize the union in the eyes of [his] fellow prisoners, as well as the prison's staff. He thought that it would be a good idea if the union could obtain official status by the North Carolina state government. Single-handedly, Brooks drafted Articles of Incorporation, By-Laws, and a Purpose and Goals Statement. . . . On September 27, 1974, the state of North Carolina officially accepted his paperwork and incorporated the union."[26]

Outside organizers had little control. The new NCPLU elected a board of directors (all prisoners) and signed their names to the incorporation papers. They sought and acquired formal affiliation with the AFL-CIO. The main agenda of the NCPLU was focused on labor-related issues, not general penal reform. In this sense, it functioned more like a traditional labor union rather than a social movement organization.

There was fiery debate among organizers over the proper scope of issues appropriate to a prisoner union. For some, a focus on labor rights, and prisoners' rights more generally, was insufficient. Prison unions should be part of a wider movement for political resistance. Advocates saw the union as part and parcel of the contemporary peace movement and the wider civil rights struggle. Tibbs describes how the members of the United Prisoner Union came to split along this line.

The feats of unions during the 1970s ranged from the mundane to the spectacular, from reforming institutional policy around food and mail, for example, to organizing mass strikes across penal institutions.

A FAMILY RESEMBLANCE

I have laid in front of us three organizational forms—grievance procedures, councils, and unions—and mere snapshots at that. Compounding matters, these forms are scattered across not only different types of institutions but different regions, with different local pressures and problems. However, not only are they part of a shared reform zeitgeist; these design choices sparked a shared conversation with recurring lines of conflict.

Both in practice and in their ideal forms the three techniques invited controversy. Part of the squabble was interpretive. Paralleling the debate over lay participation in the CAP on the outside, prisoner participation invited competing accounts of the desideratum of community control. Some described prisoner participation as a way to exert leverage on particular factions within the prison such as gangs, prison officers, and nonuniformed staff. Prisoner councils in particular were seen as a means to break up patronage at the cellblock level or, minimally, to introduce a new pressure group to change relative bargaining positions of different factions. Through the prisoner council, the prison administration could potentially exert leverage on the entire social system within the prison.[27] Others focused on community control as a coordination mechanism. If top-down prison policies were failing, perhaps bottom-up policies would be successful. Grievance procedures, councils, and unions increase prisoner buy-in, the argument goes, and allow policies to better match local needs and preferences.[28]

A third view emphasized more modest reform goals. Increasing community control in prisons meant some inclusion, not full control by prisoners. The aim was to improve general conditions through prisoners' own labor and by opening a line of communication between the warden and the cellblock.[29] A smaller, fourth group focused on participation—particularly unionization—as a vehicle to mobilize prisoners into a potent pressure group. Through creative conflict, unions might act as a bulwark against the worst excesses of custody.[30] Some went as far as to see unions as a step toward large-scale decarceration.[31]

In short, the dominant interpretations of the proper ends of community control that emerged out of the wider discussion were power sharing, policy coordination, consultation, and interest group formation. It's not clear to me, however, that these are *competing* interpretations. They form a unity—a single discourse. While no individual institutional feature (say, prisoner councils) or particular interpretation (interest group formation, perhaps) captures the essence of that discourse, collectively they constitute a "family resemblance." That is, each member of the group resembles one another in some respects but not in others. Some, like Warden Baker, emphasized both policy coordination and consultation but not interest group formation. Others were less concerned with policy coordination and played up power sharing and interest group formation. And so on. That advocates' views diverged politically is less significant than the conceptual features they had in common. What tied the wider family resemblance together is a shared belief that the pathologies of prison life were, at least in part, a function of prisoners' exclusion from prison governance.

CONTROVERSY AND CRITICISM

The historical record hasn't been kind to these reform efforts. The failure of institutional reforms during the 1970s was, by most accounts, overdetermined.[32] Experiments had run their course. Administrators didn't develop organizations capable of maintaining security and meeting basic demands for services. Moreover, they neither meet demands by the legal system for visible and rational decision-making nor lived up to the reform rhetoric of prisoners' rights. The conclusion that "high-custody" forms of prison management are the most effective at stemming lawlessness and prison violence emerged as the new common sense by the end of the decade. James Jacobs, and later John DiIulio, describe the wider events of this period as an empirical demonstration of the unworkability of the rehabilitative ideal and the human relations model of management.[33] While some analysts, like Jacobs, point to specific security challenges like gangs, others emphasize a more fundamental destabilizing transition: a rapidly increasing prison population.[34] Jonathan Simon embeds the prison rebellions of the early 1970s in a wider narrative of the popular rejection of then-dominant rehabilitative approaches to criminal justice reform.[35] Both inside and outside of prison walls, community control fed into a revanchist backlash. Political elites began to privilege punitive responses that would in time form the network of programs, strategies, and institutions that contemporary commentators have come to call *mass incarceration*.[36]

What's often lost in the discussion is what, precisely, the punitive turn in US prison policy was a turn away from. For many, the rejection of community control represents an important pivot point or a lost moment for democratic reforms.[37] Knowing the historical verdict, however, shouldn't exempt the arguments offered by community control advocates and their critics from closer scrutiny. Shared empirical assumptions can be buried, reoccurring arguments and criticisms missed, and common normative commitments obscured. A variety of contemporary approaches and movements, ranging from restorative justice practices, to legal scholarship on "democratizing criminal law," to the Movement for Black Lives, among others, don't necessarily echo the debates of the 1970s, but they certainly rhyme.[38] For the debate to flourish, the conceptual underbrush must be cleared.

Practical Objections

The most direct criticism of participatory structures like prisoner councils is that they neither are safe, nor do they promote general stability. As DiIulio writes, "It is the government of the keepers, not the society of captives, that is of primary importance."[39] For him, the simple answer for improving prison conditions is the correct one: riots and violence are, in large part, symptoms of lax security, not wider social grievances or changes in the prisoner social system. And even if the etiology of prison unrest was the prisoner social system, prison administrators are simply ill-equipped to directly influence that system. Empirically, as he sees it, there is simply no evidence that participatory management is safer.[40] Citing variation in order, amenity, and service across three prison systems facing similar pressures (California, Michigan, and Texas), DiIulio argues that the weight of the evidence suggests prison managers govern best when they govern *most*. In other words, we need hierarchical, paramilitary forms of custody.

More recent work has both complicated and challenged this claim. Vesla Weaver and Amy Lerman, for example, do not find any relationship between the presence of prisoner councils and violence. Their study analyzes a larger, more complete dataset than DiIulio's on prisoner council participation, gang activity, institutional violence, and perceptions of safety.[41] In addition, a robust empirical literature on the effectiveness of participatory institutional designs, even under conditions characterized by social disorganization, has emerged over the last few decades.[42] Most persuasive, perhaps, is Skarbek's emphasis on the *quality* of goods provision and governance, whatever that governance happens to look like. When officials govern well, prisoners have little need to govern themselves. When they don't, prisoners will seek to provide their own informal alternatives.[43]

A related criticism is that community control policies are politically tricky to implement and too vulnerable to disruption. Large-scale participatory reforms like the RGC in Walla Walla, mentioned in the discussion of prisoner councils, require a number of initial conditions that are difficult to find. As Ann Chih Lin notes, implementing programs successfully requires an understanding of how the organizational context of each individual prison will interact with the written policies that govern a particular reform program.[44] Moreover, skeptics suggest that prisoner participation simply asks too much of administrators, staff, and prisoners themselves.

Many of the designs described earlier require staff to work in multiple roles—guard, counselor, coordinator—for which they, without resources and training, are unprepared. Worse, participatory structures can become sites of power struggles among prisoner factions and between prisoners and prison officers. Along those lines, some see prisoner councils as direct descendants of the con-boss system. Participatory schemes are more susceptible to staff resistance and co-optation by other forces on the outside, such as street gangs.[45]

Likewise, critics argue the inevitable result of widespread prisoner participation is not merely internal instability but disequilibrium with external political pressures. To implement and sustain significant reform requires high-level political support, as well as the cooperation of officials in the relevant federal or state agency.[46] Or if not cooperation, then benign neglect. This, many argue, puts participatory reforms on an uneasy footing. Prison administrators and their political patrons are not politically insulated. As a consequence, they face a number of complications in managing outside public opinion.[47]

Some take this insulation argument even further. *Any* lay public involvement, inside or out, is misguided. The institutions and moral intuitions democracies use to respond to lawbreaking, they suggest, tend to make matters worse. For one, the public's tendency toward anger and revenge degrades punishment and care. When confronted with criminal violence, popular responses are rarely measured. For another, populist anger undermines the basic civil rights and liberties that we've come to expect in liberal-democratic regimes. That is, not only are responses potentially irrational, but public influence risks undermining the very conditions that sustain civil society in the first place.

While this view has risen to the level of common sense in many circles, as I've argued elsewhere, the evidence used to support it is overstated.[48] Effective insulation from lay opinion or partisanship requires a number of empirical conditions that may or may not be present, such as public trust in experts and second-order insulation (insulating the institutions that determine the rules and procedures of that institution). Not only are these factors rarely all present, particularly in the United States, but these conditions are subject to decay over time.[49] As a result, the label *insulationist* grants too much to its advocates; their position is probably better described as *technocratic*.

In practice, this means the actual choice is not between insulation and integration but between different forms of integration with public opinion. Haphazard participation, or decayed forms of insulating institutions, risks producing worse outcomes than either strict insulation or unmediated lay participation. Likewise, the arguments offered by skeptics concerning administrative complexity are not decisive, nor are they unique to community control. Any ambitious reform agenda is sure to meet similar difficulties.

While advocates may be too optimistic in their expectations for community control programs, none of the practical difficulties articulated by critics appear to be insurmountable. It's true that the administrative burden of implementing community control-inspired programs might at times outweigh the desire for greater ward participation. A procedure or process that can't secure the basic needs of the group (for example) is worse than useless; it's wasteful. However, it is not clear, a priori, how that balance should be struck.

Philosophical Objections

The debate over community control in custody didn't stop with concerns about effective policy delivery or the role of public accountability. Others expressed more foundational objections. *Even if* it's possible to implement participatory reforms in a tractable way, we ought not to. It's on this register that the tensions described in the previous two chapters resurface.

One objection, from the political left, charged community control with being a palliative—mere "reformism," in the pejorative sense of that term. An influential version of this criticism is that custody, by its very nature, is fundamentally incompatible with social progress. Angela Davis offers a useful example. In the 1990s the warden of the San Francisco County Jail was a strong women's rights advocate, and the program director had spent eight years as a prisoner in San Quentin. By this reform regime's own account, the ideal endpoint of reform ought to be to turn the jail into a kind of mandatory community college that requires students to take courses while incarcerated (including topics such as sexual violence, AIDS workshops, and nonheterosexual lifestyles). This aspiration is as old as the prison and continues to inspire activists and scholars.[50] At first glance this seems like a reasonable and potentially empowering institutional transformation. However, Davis argues, this environment would simply reclothe prison officers in school teachers' garb. The disempowering effects of control and discipline would simply transfer to a classroom setting.

Davis writes that examples such as the one offered here "point to the inability of the prison system to contain any kind of progressive change. The walls will not allow for it. The walls are always there. So that even when you try to move things forward, you end up in a place that is very authoritarian, a place in which the women and men who are there are not respected as human beings."[51]

The "walls" Davis describes are more than concrete and steel; they are the norms and procedures of custody itself that are beyond contest. This argument echoes those of a number of others, including David Rothman, who claim that custody inevitably results in a trade-off between conscience and convenience. The best-laid custodial designs, even when paired with recognizably democratic or humanitarian values, confront an inertia toward decay.

While Davis's wider abolitionist project remains compelling, a part of the argument is stated too strongly.[52] While we should rightly reject putting new paint on dungeon walls and calling it reform, that does not mean that custody is irreconcilable with democracy. A world without prisons—a world worth striving for—need *not* be a world without punishment, trusteeship, or paternalistic care. Those latter elements, whatever institutional form they are given, appear to be inextricable from any plausible theory of democracy. The case for the abolition of punishment itself stands on much shakier philosophical ground than the claim that prisons should be abolished as a form of punishment.[53]

A second version of this objection came from the failure of the larger movement for community control in the War on Poverty. It gets closer to specifying precisely why, to use Davis's language, custody resists "any kind of progressive change." In this view community control is an example of a wider tendency to treat democracy simply as an organizational design problem. When equipped with the right tools, a careful architect can create a set of institutions *on behalf of* a marginalized group that will allow that group to realize its interests. Cruikshank calls this belief the "will to empower," and the belief crossed party lines.[54] Both the political Right and the Left in this period understood "the poor" to be insufficiently self-governing. On the right, the aim of empowerment was to form rational economic and entrepreneurial actors. On the left, the goal was to generate political self-advocacy and resistance. While institutional prescriptions varied, the end desire was similar: to motivate the poor to act on their own, *true* interests.

Without more context, however, it is unclear how much weight to give this criticism. It's uncontroversial that "participatory" institutional designs can forward paternalistic or authoritarian ends in custody, just as hierarchical decision-making structures can be put in the service of democratic values. This observation is, in an alternative form, a restatement of familiar critiques of strictly procedural accounts of democratic politics.[55] One basic response is to note that community control entails a commitment to particular values, not just a set of decision-making procedures. That is, a shared moral vision, not simply an organizational technique, might ground the optimism of reformers that democratic values, institutional design, and human capability can form a virtuous cycle of progressive social change.

THE LIMITS OF COMMUNITY

Admittedly, I've moved hastily through the core arguments. Here, however, I'm less interested in defending community control as a comprehensive program. My purpose lies elsewhere. The confusions, criticisms, and responses sketched earlier bring into relief a number of shared normative assumptions, in addition to a series of recurring empirical disputes. I have worked from the premise that an underbrush of partially articulated concepts can choke the growth of debate around more contemporary iterations of these reform ideas, which, to be clear, I think are ideas worthy of debate.

That said, I'm less certain what to make of the political theory shouldering the tradition of community control in custody. Even if critics of community control are too pessimistic in their assessments of participation in custody, one might worry that those who embrace the community control model careen too far in the other direction. In theory, those in custody can both influence, and be influenced by, the institutions tasked with their confinement and care. Yet even a cursory reading of the history of community control efforts suggests otherwise. Prisoner participation more often seems shaped by, than shapes, the beliefs, institutional dynamics, and problem-solving strategies of the institutions of which they are part. Sorting out the reasons takes us back to the exclusion thesis. Community control advocates tend to *bound* "crime" and its correlates. They locate both the causes and solutions to criminality in prisoners themselves. The result is policy making that does not require any adjustment by those on the outside. And community control *without* a wider redistribution of resources risks becoming yet another corrosive self-help philosophy.[56]

A wider ebb and flow come into focus: the erosion of custodial authority is met with an attempt to canalize wards' struggle for recognition in a way that shores up, not challenges, the status quo. That attempt, of course, can fail. The prisoner council at Charlestown penitentiary, one of the examples mentioned in passing earlier, provides an opportunity to concretize this otherwise abstract pattern.

CHARLESTOWN

At Charlestown, 566 prisoners began a sit-down strike in the spring of 1946. Strikers were protesting harsh parole board decisions, but their concerns were broader. Charlestown had been in operation for almost a century and a half; it was a dungeon both metaphorically and literally. A year before the strike, the Massachusetts commissioner of corrections even described the conditions at the prison as "filthy" and "not fit for dogs," and he castigated prior administrations for allowing the facility to fall into such disrepair.[57]

In the wake of the strike, Lewis Lawes, a governor-appointed expert, delivered his report that the parole board's recommendations were, in fact, too severe, and advised that the dilapidated Charlestown prison facility be closed entirely. Plans were made for the construction of a new prison to replace it, but action on those plans was slow. Ground wouldn't be broken on a new facility near Walpole, Massachusetts, for another four years. Malcolm X would spend the initial years of his incarceration at Charlestown during this liminal period before being transferred to the Norfolk Prison Colony which, in his words, was "comparatively, a heaven."[58]

Citing the Lawes report, the newly formed prisoner grievance committee at Charlestown asked Governor Maurice Tobin to correct past parole board injustices. While a few token measures had been implemented, again, the pace of policy change was plodding. An open letter published three years later in the *Mentor* (the prison's newspaper) criticized the state parole board. It noted the forty-six prisoner-led protests against the parole board and emphasized that despite the recommendations of the expert investigation led by Lawes, no reforms of consequence had been made. Later that year, the newly-appointed head of the state parole board met with Charlestown prisoners. In response to mounting pressure, he publicly promised that the grievance committee's recommendations would be taken into account.[59]

The troubles swelling at Charlestown were part of a wider wave of protests, stoppages, and revolts sweeping across the nation's aging prison system.[60] In July 1952 smaller disturbances built to a crescendo: a mass uprising at Charlestown. A number of prisoners, some reportedly already on strike in the laundry shop, took three hostages. Among the prisoners' grievances and demands were the following:

1. Bad and insufficient food.
2. 17 hours of cell confinement out of 24.
3. No pay for prison work.
4. Poor personal sanitation provisions (each prisoner allowed one shower a week, for six minutes a man, on Saturday).
5. No hearing before a prisoner is placed in detention cell on mere complaint of another inmate.
6. Poor facilities for washing clothes.
7. A more favorable schedule of allotting time off for good behavior.
8. Time off for good behavior for lifers.
9. More liberal mail and visiting privileges for prisoners in special detention.
10. More liberal parole policies.[61]

The commissioner and warden negotiated with prisoners face to face with various reporters in attendance. Prisoners maintained order during the negotiations, caucused at half-hour intervals among themselves, and eventually voted to surrender.

As a part of that negotiation, the existing ad hoc grievance committee was made into a more formal advisory council under an agreement referred to as the "inmate council constitution." The details of that constitution will sound familiar. Like the patient federation at St. Elizabeths discussed in the previous chapter, the council had a representative structure. Each cellblock could, by a two-thirds vote, elect one prisoner to the council. The entire population then elected six men from the council to be councilors; the remainder were designated as representatives. The six councilors were tasked with electing a chairman to be the overall representative of the institution, who would serve a six-month term in office. Together with the editor of the prison newspaper, who was regarded as the council public relations officer, the councilors met with the warden to review and discuss matters referred by the full council. The chairman also appointed one or more representatives to various committees approved by the warden: finance (commissary), sports, entertainment, library, kitchen, and avocational. The duty of each committee was to observe and report in writing to the full council any complaints or suggestions prisoners wished presented to the warden during the monthly meetings. The council issued public statements, communicated with the administration during work stoppages, and was a vehicle to organize prisoner grievances.[62]

By 1955 the wider Massachusetts Department of Correction was in disarray. *Time Magazine* offers a grim image:

> The Massachusetts State Prison, a cramped compound of blackened granite and dilapidated brick buildings in the Charlestown section of Boston, is the oldest, most disreputable prison in the U.S. It was built in 1805, has been damned for 80 years as a verminous pesthole, unfit for human habitation.
>
> In the past two years the prison has been the scene of 16 disorders, including riots and attempted escapes. Last week, in the 17th and most spectacular try, four armed convicts held five guards and six fellow prisoners hostage, and kept the combined forces of the National Guard and prison authorities at bay for 82 hours, the second-longest prison siege in history (the longest: 100 hours, in 1952, at the State Prison of Southern Michigan, at Jackson). Scene of the attempted break was the Detention Demerit Building, popularly known as Cherry Hill, where the prison's most unruly criminals are kept.[63]

In the wake of near constant disruption, disorder, and rebellion, the governor appointed a special commission to study the Massachusetts penal system and named the president of Tufts University, Nils Wessel, as chair.[64]

The use of grievance committees, and their formalization into institutionally recognized "inmate advisory councils," as we have seen, was not unique to Charlestown. It was part and parcel of a wider penal management philosophy that was slowly coming into vogue throughout the 1950s. It was in line with newer, rehabilitative approaches to prison and hospital reform that also provided ideological cover for administrative objectives ranging from riot control, to cost reduction, to the management of ward labor. Testament to the strength of the council idea at Charlestown is that the much-respected Wessel commission actually *rejected* the idea of a prisoner council among its proposed reforms, yet the council persisted. After Charlestown closed its doors for the last time in 1956, the prisoner council was reconstituted at the newly built Massachusetts Institute of Correction, Walpole. For the next decade the prisoner council at Walpole served the general functions sketched earlier. Prisoner consultation served as a pressure valve for dissent, made grievances legible (and thus more manageable) to the administration, and helped coordinate prison policy.

The period between 1965 and 1975, however, marked a fundamental transition both at Walpole and beyond. America was on fire. The peak of violence during this period was from the summer of 1967 to the 137 separate incidents that followed the assassination of Martin Luther King Jr. the following April. As Elizabeth Hinton notes, public memory of these incidents on the street largely stops in 1968, even though regular rebellions continued for years afterward. In her accounting, some 960 communities across the United States witnessed 1,949 uprisings; 40,000 people were arrested, 10,000 were injured, and at least 220 were killed.[65] Rebellions on the streets were paired with stoppages, strikes, and revolts on cellblocks. In 1967 there were five such events; there were fifteen in 1968, twenty-seven in 1970, thirty-seven in 1971, and forty-eight in 1972.[66] The events at Walpole, as I detail in the next chapter, were simply a drop in this larger rainstorm.

Two decades before, in the early 1950s, a tidal wave of prison rebellions failed to dislodge an optimism among policy elites that prisons could contribute to the common good. At prisons like Charlestown, faith in therapeutic interventions was rattled but not broken. This time, however, was different.[67] The ambitions of reformers were rejected: so many dreams collapsed, so many experiments abandoned. In the spring of 1973 the nagging question of who governs was again thrust into the limelight. Unlike in the 1950s, attempts to canalize prisoner protest failed. The sluices cracked. Energized by the social currents of the day, the prisoners at Walpole rejected what they took to be pseudo or Potemkin forms of participation. They refused the prison administration's attempt to revive a multilevel grievance committee, they gutted the influence of the inmate advisory council, and they eventually disbanded that council entirely. They came to embrace a radicalized vision of community control, a vision of prison democracy that remixed the ideals of earlier reformers.

Enter the Walpole rebellion.

CHAPTER 5

On Prison Democracy

At approximately 10:00 a.m. on March 14, 1973, a volunteer civilian observer noted that high-ranking officials from the prison officers' union were gathering at the entrance of the Massachusetts Correctional Institution at Walpole (MCI-Walpole), a maximum security prison about fifteen miles outside of Boston.[1] Rumors had been circulating for days within the prison that the officers were going to strike.[2] A few hours later, the entire day shift of prison officers called in sick.[3] Rev. Ed Rodman, the head of the civilian observer program, remembers: "That morning, I had set up a table after the first shift of observers went in. We let the second shift in at three and I was sitting at the table. One of the guards came up to me with a big manila envelope. He dropped it on the desk with a big clunk, saying, 'I think these belong to you.' In the envelope was every key to the prison."[4] The prisoners were now running the asylum, so to speak.

At the time, Walpole was the most violent prison in Massachusetts, perhaps even the most violent in the country.[5] Murders were frequent, stabbings even more so. In the week leading up to the strike, observers noted again and again that both prisoners and officers lived under psychologically stressful conditions of fear and uncertainty. Compounding matters, the physical conditions inside the prison were intolerable: as a result of both protest and neglect, many cell blocks were ankle-deep in trash and corridor walls were stained with feces and urine.[6]

INSIDE—Robert Dellelo (center) addresses yester-   Inmates (left) and two members of Prisoners Union of
day's news conference while two fellow Walpole   California listen. (Globe Photo by Tom Landers)

Inmates challenge DA to shakedown

~y Stephen Wermiel   side Walpole during the   politicians would get out   day for 180 guards and 25

FIGURE 5. A photo in an article published in the *Boston Globe* on April 10, 1973, during the prison officer strike at Massachusetts Correctional Institution at Walpole. *Source*: *Boston Globe* photo by Tom Landers.

That afternoon, Commissioner John Boone declared a state of emergency.[7] The state police were sent to the gates of the prison. The prison officers' union was in a protracted dispute with the Department of Corrections, headed by the recently appointed commissioner.[8] The union hoped the mass sick leave and ensuing breakdown of security would draw negative media publicity to the Boone administration's policies.[9] Boone, conversely, saw the strike as an opportunity to break the prison officers' union, which he saw as standing in the way of implementing large-scale prison reform in Massachusetts.[10] Boone took a risk. Instead of sending in the state police, he turned over the management of the prison to the newly formed and elected prisoners' union (the Walpole chapter of the National Prisoner Reform Association, the NPRA), a skeleton crew of officers and trainees from other institutions, and civilian observers.

Between March 15 and May 19, the NPRA was the central force governing the prisoners at Walpole. There were no murders and little violence, and the prisoners ran the kitchen and foundry, maintained security, deliberated over policy and action, and negotiated with the prison administration.[11] During this time civilian observers were continuously present in the institution, logging over ten thousand hours inside Walpole.[12] These volunteers informally interviewed prisoners and recorded various events that took place. The handwritten notes of the observers are not easily accessible, and no academic attention has yet been paid to them.[13] One observer described the process of interpreting his own experience within the prison as "trying to drink from a fire hose," and that description also aptly characterizes my experience reading through the observers' notes. The observer files contain historical fragments in raw form: torn scraps of paper, sometimes dated, sometimes not; typewritten drafts of reports authored by the Ad Hoc Committee; observer program rosters, recruitment fliers, and draft press releases; and a host of other documents, many of which are annotated, left by the NPRA during the 1970s. Scattered among a dozen musty filing boxes in a closet in Cambridge, Massachusetts, is a hastily created archive of a prison reform movement in full swing.

The historiography that exists on Walpole, while both limited and controversial, is embroiled in a philosophical conflict over what it means in a democracy for a group to become an object of care or custody. For some, the events at Walpole are exemplars of Hobbesian anarchy and bureaucratic failure.[14] This account usually takes one of two forms, either a call to increase law and order within prisons or a push to reallocate goods and services to the task of treatment. In other words, prisoner participation is understood as a symptom of a failed treatment or control regimen. I call this extension of the standard view the *divided* narrative. However, an alternative account emerges from a close reading of the Walpole episode. In this narrative Walpole is an experiment in participatory democracy and community control.[15] I call this less familiar view the *united* narrative.[16]

What are we to make of these two narratives? The present chapter offers some answers, drawing upon the archival documents and oral histories left by the prisoners, observers, and staff at Walpole. Unlike its divided counterpart, the united narrative was never systematically enunciated. However, as I detail in the following, its central principles can be reconstructed from a close reading of the tumultuous events of that spring in 1973. The final pages forward the claim that both views are insufficient, and that both views continue to shape our legal and moral imagination about custody.

MARCH 15 TO MAY 18, 1973

You've got to have rules and you're not dealing with rational people.
These are men who have usually been unable to accept the word
"NO." I tell an inmate to do something and he tells me "fuck you!"
I write a disciplinary report on him, but there's no administration
response. There is a total breakdown in order here.

*We want a prison community as cool as the street. We want a voice
in our prison "society." Treat us like men and we'll act like men.*

By March 16, the day after the strike, the media coverage was constant
and its pitch shrill. Newscasts reported that Walpole was in chaos and
that "drunk" and "drug-addled" prisoners were roaming around the
prison. The observers inside the prison, however, tell a different story. It
can be expressed in a series of words: "calm," "relaxed," "joy."[17] This is in
contrast to observer reports from the previous week of high tension and
repeated impressions that "the place could blow" at any time. Almost
every observer present that day noted high levels of unity among the
prisoners. "The atmosphere in the prison was almost that of a Roman
holiday. Much bustling back and forth, noisy talking and good humored
jostling. All the cell block doors were open and the men roamed about
freely in the hall."[18]

There was an outpouring of political talk inside in the prison, particularly during those first few weeks after the strike. Both prisoners
and observers felt they were witnessing history in the making.[19] Some,
like the infamous Albert DeSalvo, focused on the potential power of the
prisoners' union: "They don't know what we've got here. Rhode Island's
prisons are unionized; we're unionized; Norfolk . . . Concord . . . Ver-
mont. We'll be able to call a national prison strike."[20] A few turned to
discussions of class and race, noting that most of the prisoners at Walpole were poor or had a working-class background, that a large number
of prisoners were Black, and that "richer people would get off for what
they did. . . . [M]ost of the men admitted that they were guilty of crimes
and deserved to be punished, but the fact that others consistently got
off . . . built a strong resentment in them."[21] And others focused on the
potential of the union to push for smaller remedies within the prison,
from fixing the heating system to providing basic vocational training:
"The NPRA is fighting with the administration. But I'm fighting another battle. I see that yard out there. It's being used for nothing. They
could just put a single story building there, away from the fence, and
how many fucking classrooms could they put there? We're not asking
for any silver platter, or ladder to get out of here. Give me the tools and
I'll work and compete in the society I'm supposed to live in. I'll build
my own ladder."[22]

Over time the torrent of conversation did slow, but it never stopped.[23]

The civilian observers recorded hundreds upon hundreds of prisoner
ideas, suggestions, and comments concerning prison reform, both at

Walpole and beyond. Perusing the notes of the observers, one is struck not only by the creativity of many of the proposed reforms, but also by the sheer number of ideas.[24] Prisoners cared. The simple possibility of having a seat at the bargaining table, by some accounts, was a motor for prisoner deliberation and expression.

The presence of observers inside the prison, of course, shaped what was said and how it was said. For one, having members of the community on hand—young and old, and from various walks of life—who were willing and eager to listen offered encouragement and validation to prisoner political expression. For another, civilian observers produced classic "observer effects"; both prisoners and guards tried to play to their audience. Michael Ignatieff, who during this time was working on his dissertation research that would eventually culminate in *A Just Measure of Pain: The Penitentiary in the Industrial Revolution 1750–1850*, noted in one of his reports moments of "rather unreal politeness and cooperation between inmates and guards, unreal because neither side conceals for long its real contempt for each other. . . . [B]oth sides play a sort of subtle charade for the benefit of the observers."[25]

Beyond the initial euphoria of having control of the prison and the outpouring of conversation, the observers noted a deeper level of unity ("unprecedented solidarity," "a truly remarkable esprit de corps," a "pride in con-unity") among the prisoners.[26] Observers noted that prisoners were not just united because of a mutual hatred of the "screws" (slang for regular prison officers), but also because of a widely held sense of shared political purpose.[27] In a speech given to the general prison population a day after the prison officer walkout, NPRA external board member Obalaji Rust "firmly spoke informing the inmates of the one thing they all had in common: They were all[,] all of them[,] Black, White, or Puerto Rican[,] oppressed and that the guards were also oppressed. But the only way the prisoners can aid in bringing about prison reform is by getting their shit together. Any differences they may have among each other would have to be overlooked, because only by sticking together could they come out on top. Otherwise, they'd go down the drain."[28] Rust received a standing ovation from the prisoners both when he entered the assembly hall and when he left.[29] The prisoners were under no illusion that this period of self-rule would last. Most expected self-rule to end in violence; references to the Attica rebellion two years earlier are peppered throughout the observer reports.[30] Prisoners believed that their fates were linked.

On individual cellblocks this cohesion took a variety of forms. Murders, stabbings, and sexual violence stopped; membership on the various NPRA committees ballooned; and as mentioned earlier, observers captured in their notes a flood of fragments of everyday conversations about local politics. Prisoners engaged in various protest behaviors, from work stoppages, to hunger strikes, to collective resistance, to "behavioral modification" tactics on the disciplinary blocks.[31] And organizations like Black African Nations Toward Unity (BANTU) and the Muslim Brotherhood were integral to political consciousness raising among Black prisoners.[32]

This solidarity persisted for over two months; from March 15, the day of the officer walkout, to May 19, the day the state police took control of Walpole, general group cohesion was maintained among the approximately 560 prisoners at Walpole.[33] And it is this solidarity that prisoners, observers, and trainee cadets credit as a condition of possibility for NPRA governance. It's important to note that this solidarity was not a logical outcome of the prison environment; quite the opposite, the observer reports highlight a series of splits that had to be mended, or at least papered over, to make unity possible.

Two obstacles in particular stand out in the notes: the convict code and ethno-racial conflict. I briefly describe each in turn.

A central inertial force moving against unity was the hegemony of the "convict code" in the prisoner population. With maxims that include "do your own time" and "don't snitch" and warnings to stay away from "lowriders"—those convicts engaged in interpersonal disputes—the convict code doesn't exactly lend itself to collective action. The backbone of the convict code is the logic of social order; while atomistic, it provides a means to resolve disputes, assign status, and maintain dignity in a difficult and uncertain environment. As I describe in more detail later, the convict code was revised but not abandoned in the new social order established after the walkout.

The second obstacle, ethno-racial conflict, warrants a bit more attention. For one, the postracial vision of collective resistance so eloquently articulated by Obalaji Rust (described earlier) downplays the significance of racial politics at Walpole after the walkout. Observers recorded, for example, that prisoners largely self-segregated by ethnicity during chow and that the vast majority of recreational activities were uniracial.[34] Additionally, the freedom to move between cells on each block resulted in racially homogeneous enclaves within the prison.[35] However, even if claims of cross-racial solidarity among the prisoners were exaggerated, or aspirational, given the context even a minimal level of cooperation is difficult to fathom. For one, the vast majority of prisoners at MCI-Walpole came from the Boston area, and the streets of Boston during the early 1970s were entangled in gang politics between the Irish and Italian mobs.[36] While this did not entail open conflict inside the prison, it meant that like neighborhoods on the outside, the prison community was largely divided into groups with discrete spheres of influence.[37]

Furthermore, racial tensions in the city of Boston were high; just one year after the Walpole strike, Boston would be mired in open conflict over compulsory busing aimed at desegregating the schools of Massachusetts.[38] Prisons are embedded in a wider community, and shifts in that wider community play out in the prison in complex ways.[39] The New York State Special Commission on Attica described the relationship as follows:

> For the black inmate in Attica, the atmosphere on September 8, 1971, was not unlike that in the cities before the holocausts of Harlem, Watts, Newark, and Detroit. Sit-ins, demonstrations, and petitions had been met with excuses, delays, and repression. Organized, peaceful efforts had been rebuffed or ignored. Inmates and guards alike later commented, "The tension was so thick around here you could cut it with a knife." No organizers were necessary; no plans were required; no leaders needed. As in the cities in 1967, the situation itself was explosive. All that was needed was a spark to set it off.[40]

Drawing on the arguments of the Attica Commission, a group of public policy researchers make the point that wider social conflicts likely played a significant role in undermining traditional prisoner-staff relations at Walpole prison.[41]

In addition, racial tension within the Massachusetts Department of Corrections complicated matters. Governor Francis Sargent appointed John O. Boone commissioner of the Department of Corrections just a few months before the prison officers' strike. Boone was the first African American commissioner in the state's history, and he was tasked with reforming a bureaucracy that was almost all white. Like most prisons in the country during this time, the vast majority of prison officers were white, and officers would regularly leverage the racial prejudices of the prisoner population as a management technique.

The tension between racism and solidarity at Walpole is nicely evinced in the following vignette provided in one observer's notes:

> In my block (5) there was a white guy who during the course of a conversation said to a black man, "Go do this for me, we brought you over

to be slaves anyway." A very dangerous thing to say, so I thought. Later on, . . . [a man in the next cell over] pleaded with me to listen carefully to what he was saying . . . : "Sure, they (we, everyone probably) are racist and prejudiced, and when the cons can't get over that they play games. But these men are brothers underneath all that. Brothers in a deeper sense than most people ever experience, because their love for each other is constantly being tested."[42]

Racially charged language was hardly exceptional; the observers captured both moments of cross-racial cooperation and fragments of racial anxiety.

Yet despite these fissures and frictions the prisoners stood together in the spring of 1973. But what did self-rule look like? First, consider the formal structure. The internal board of the NPRA, the leaders of the prisoner union, consisted of twenty-one seats. The seats were divided by race: "nine Whites, nine Blacks, and three Spanish."[43] The individuals that filled each seat were selected by their own ethnic or racial group and were, by various accounts, the notables within the institution.[44] In each cellblock there was an elected block representative or "block captain" who was responsible for managing any issues that arose on the block. In addition, there were thirty-some committees, overseen by the internal board, which managed particular features of prison life: a kitchen committee, an education committee, a Black problems committee, and a hospital committee, among a slew of others.

The various committees of the NPRA forwarded multiple purposes. On the one hand, they made decentralized governance possible. The internal board did not have the capacity to respond to every issue that arose in the prisoner population, but various committees could develop task-specific competencies. On the other hand, encouraging participation was a way to co-opt potentially fractious elements in the population. And most importantly, committees provided a way for prisoners that didn't care about politics to contribute to self-rule. Robert Dellelo, the president of the NPRA, explains: "Guys who knew the hospital would get assigned there; guys that worked in the kitchen would get assigned there. What we did with the committees, what I tried to do, was find the guys who were sincerely interested in the area and put them in the area. For example, Jimmy Pena did not give a fuck about prison reform; he wanted to get a good meal and to be treated like a decent human being. He was on the Kitchen Committee."[45] One effect of this approach was that management of everyday tasks became integral to the philosophy of self-rule espoused by the prisoner population;

cleaning floors, for example, became an affirmation of dignity and autonomy.

Any committee could call a general assembly of the prisoner population for deliberation and a vote, and attendance at these assemblies would range between fifty and five hundred prisoners. The mood of wider deliberative assemblies ranged from sedate to cantankerous, but they were largely civil. If an inmate was intoxicated or threatened another inmate, he was told to leave. Everyone who wanted time to speak on an issue was granted it, and decisions were ultimately reached via a voice vote or a public show of hands.[46] The assemblies were used to bring major issues to the prisoner population; the vast majority of day-to-day business was conducted within committees or by the internal board.

The formal structure of NPRA governance was the child of a negotiated truce among various factions at the beginning of the prison officers' strike. One observer wrote: "Several inmates told me that there are many inmate conflicts that are being put aside during this crisis—and that when the crisis ends, there will be more stabbings, beatings, and murders."[47] Robert Dellelo remembers:

> The racial tension in the prison was thick. Black Power was bouncing. What happened is I said, "There is only one color and that is blue." The guards wore khaki, which was brown; the prisoners were wearing blue. It was blue versus brown. "You are either blue or brown. There is no in-between ground. We are all in this together." . . . I explained to everyone, "We can't have no more beefs for six months. We have to agree no beefs. Everyone backs off." The question was, "What if someone nails someone during that truce, what happens?" My answer was, "Anyone who violates the truce, we will take him down." And they knew I would and could. We had the hard core on call, so even if I couldn't take someone down myself, I had someone to do it. That made a lot of people feel very, very safe. The guards could not work us like before. If we refused to fight each other, they lost a lot of their power. There was a peace across the prison that never was there before.[48]

This negotiated truce created a credible alternative to the existing social order. Beyond a guarantee of security, each ethnic group had to ensure that they kept "their house clean"—that is, that they would refuse to allow "stoolies" (as in stool pigeons, informers) and "molesters" (sex offenses involving children) into their ranks.[49] The truce was a reimagining of, but not a departure from, the basic tenets of the convict code.[50]

The norms around this truce, however, did not uniformly prohibit violence. If two people had a conflict, and both parties were about equal size, then it was fine that they squared off: "The word was that if there was to be a showdown between him and the one he allegedly stabbed that it would be 'one on one' and if anyone entered in to it that the one who interfered would get it. . . . The population would enforce this."[51] After the fight, the two should "shake hands, smoke a joint, and move on." The idea was to contain conflict, to prevent small fires from turning into blazes.

Most minor incidents, like petty theft, were addressed by appeals to solidarity, mixed with embarrassing the rule breaker in front of his peers on the block: "We educated the cons into not ripping off their brothers, because we are ripped off by the system. . . . [I]f a con rips off another con for his personal belongings he becomes what the system is, he becomes a pig, and so we educate the cons into not becoming pigs."[52] However, calls to solidarity were also backed up, if need be, with harsher discipline: "Prisoner who had been transferred from Norfolk because of his petty stealing, started stealing things from prisoners at Walpole (towels, food, etc.). Last night a group of inmates caught him in the gym and beat him up. Wanted to teach him a lesson." Similarly, a prisoner on the hospital committee suspected of stealing medicine was booted from his position and ended up with a black eye.[53] Other examples are scattered throughout various observer reports.[54]

The NPRA formed a tactical committee, headed by Ralph Hamm and Larry Rooney, which shouldered the herculean task of maintaining order in the prison.[55] Remember, once again, that despite a prisoner population that had significant access to weapons, no stabbings or murders took place during those two months.[56] One incident recorded by two observers is particularly illustrative of how a small conflict can snowball. After a fight among three men, two Black prisoners and one white,

> a white man came down . . . . He mingled with the blacks. Talk was alternately accusing and indifferent. Place nearly full now. Eventually someone hit someone and the white and a black faced off. Almost immediately both drew large, heavy machete-type knives. This made it hard for the others (who displayed no like weapons) to come between them. I and [F] moved outside the door. They were going to cut each other's heads off. Much movement inside. Somehow the fight was averted. It seemed to me that at the end the white group just walked away. About 100–200 must have been there.[57]

Talking with prisoners the next day, another observer reported that the initial incident, the conflict among the three men, was understood to be "a personal beef and not any type of racial outbreak." While incidents like this are exceptional in the observer files, moments like the one just cited reveal an important general point. Simple deterrence was not enough to guarantee security; order at Walpole required both an ability and a *desire* to deescalate conflict among the major factions within the prison.[58]

In all, the scope of governance touched almost all facets of prison life during this time: dispensing of medicine, dispute resolution, recreation, outside visitors, food distribution, even the daily block counts. Creating a credible social order also bought the NPRA leverage in negotiations with the prison administration and made the call for prisoner unionization credible. On May 18, with Boone's blessing, the acting superintendent of the prison decided to bring in the state police and lock down Walpole. Observers were expelled from the prison for a week, and when they were allowed to return, they were only permitted selective access to the institution. On June 10, the observer program was disbanded.

"THE INMATES ARE RUNNING THE PRISON"

The politics of participation at Walpole prison is probably not what democratic theorists would create in a vacuum. As others have elaborated, the government of "liberated spaces" can entail practices of discipline that some might find bizarre or distasteful.[59] The facts related to prisoner self-rule shaped but did not determine how the Walpole episode was narrated. Consider this reflection by a civilian observer: "Strange, what different meanings can attach to the phrase 'the inmates are running the prison.' A number of men said this to me in a quiet, undefiant way, to indicate that they are assuming responsibility for some the routines . . . formerly carried out by guards. The inmates are in effect maintaining order. I imagine that what the guard was trying to convey to me by his reference to the 'present situation' was that the inmates had taken over something vital that belonged to the guards."[60]

Two dominant narratives were used to interpret the events at Walpole: the divided narrative and the united narrative.[61]

The Divided Narrative

The divided narrative of prison reform is closely aligned with the second interpretation of the phrase "the inmates are running the prison" just described. For those primarily concerned with the distribution of goods, with providing order, amenity, and service, prisoner self-rule at Walpole was, at best, a haphazard attempt to muddle through in the face of maladroit management by the Massachusetts Department of Corrections.

A significant amount of the newspaper coverage of those turbulent months takes this approach, and elements of case study presented earlier surely can be shoehorned into this narrative. One *Boston Globe* journalist made this point using an officer's perspective: "'Who runs Walpole? The inmates? I don't know who else is,' Officer Arthur Dunn said. 'They're getting tired of running the place. They have problems, medical problems, drug problems. They don't want to handle the junkies either.'"[62] The leader of the prison officers' union cast the problems of prisoner governance in more stark terms: "[McLaughlin] said the 'permissive policy' instituted by [State Secretary] Goldmark and [Commissioner] Boone has given control of the prisons to 'the scum of the inmate population.' He said he was not referring to the 98 percent of the inmates who 'are no problem. They want to do their time and go home.'"[63] From this perspective prisoner self-governance was mob rule, in both senses of the term *mob*.[64]

The politicians and administrators who initially supported Commissioner Boone offered a similar diagnosis. The Walpole situation was about program implementation and bureaucratic politics, not political recognition. Boone's management style, his attempt to sidestep (or step over) the concerns of prison officers, and a racially toxic institutional climate all but ensured conflict and disorder.[65] The fracas at Walpole was ultimately seen as a distraction to a wider correctional reform agenda.[66] Among these elites, officer and prisoner strikes were viewed as a kind of growing pain, a symptom of a treatment regime in transition.

One of the clearest and most thoughtful expositions of this wider divided narrative is John DiIulio's *Governing Prisons*.[67] Inspired by Alexis de Tocqueville and Gustave de Beaumont, DiIulio's book frames the central problem of prison reform as a problem of governance. He asks, "Is it possible for prisons to be governed at an acceptable human and financial cost?" His answer, in brief, is yes; poor prison conditions are produced by observable and remediable defects in the way that prisons are organized and managed. Specifically, he argues that "high-custody" (hierarchical, restrictive) forms of prison organization are most effective at stemming prison violence.

The frame of governance and governability in DiIulio's account is useful, and I find that the conceptual metaphor of "prison as a constitutional government" is particularly revealing.[68] At a glance, one might think that a government with subjects who have little control over the conditions of their lives is more akin to an authoritarian regime than a constitutional democracy. For DiIulio, however, the reference public that holds administrators democratically accountable is *outside* the prison, and consequently for him there is no democratic deficit created by paramilitary forms of prison management. Prisoners simply are not part of the demos, of civilized society: "Given the lawless and uncivilized character of their citizens, inmate societies ought ... to be subject to strong official controls and a tight, mandatory regime of work and programs."[69] From this interpretive perspective, it's unclear what response or recognition—as administrators, as members of public on the outside, or as prisoners—befits a group exercising voice outside the "constitutional foundation" of the prison polis. While the evidence presented in the earlier case study is not dispositive, it seems clear that something like a "participatory culture" emerged at Walpole during those early months of 1973.[70] Deliberation and democratic decision-making were prominent features of prisoner self-rule, and an election was even held. Thus the claim that prisoners' unions like NPRA are a simple example of mob rule seems untenable. In DiIulio's vision of democracy, prisoners become the "part that has no part" of a prison political order "forged by revenge and cooled by forgiveness."[71]

The concepts of governance, exclusion, and democratic accountability that delineate DiIulio's account are revealing but limited. A key difficulty is DiIulio's narrow vision of political governance. Consider three dimensions of the exercise of authority. First is governance, the procedures for collectively deciding how to deploy labor and capital. This can be distinguished from the second dimension, the task of management, the actual work of deploying, or governing, that labor and capital. And the third dimension is the legal basis of the organization's right to govern the labor and capital within its jurisdiction.[72] DiIulio is primarily concerned with the second sense of governance, governance as management. But the prisoners at Walpole, in various voices, pushed for a right to self-determination on the other two dimensions as well—pushing for inclusion in the procedures that allocate goods in the prison, and in some cases rejecting the legitimacy of custody itself.

Prisoner participation, in DiIulio's account, shares important characteristics with what social theorists over the last decade have come to call neoliberal penality. *Neoliberal penality* refers to the idea that the state should assert its "responsibility, potency, and efficiency" in crime management while "proclaiming and organizing its own impotence on the economic front."[73] This logic, according to Bernard Harcourt, is an unstated premise in contemporary discussions about prison policy, and, more controversially, acted as a "condition of possibility" for the rise of mass incarceration in the United States over the last four decades.[74] In *Governing Prisons* we see a parallel configuration, a civil society of freely contracting individuals and an authoritarian prison society composed of the unruly and unreasonable. Here, however, the lynchpin is not the "natural order" described by Harcourt that justifies laissez-faire economic policies; instead, it's a largely implicit democratic theory of custody, a theory built on democratic exclusions and reference publics.

My aim is not simply to suggest that Walpole exposes a tension between the real and the represented, though the observer files definitely suggest descriptive insufficiencies in the divided narrative. Nor is my goal to draw out the friction between a particular narrative form and the enactment of that form, though the distance between the two certainly can tell us about our enduring identifications and affective attachments. Rather, my point is to highlight how the divided narrative can, without contradiction, omit from discussion the forms of need and political exclusion human beings experience behind prison walls.

Unlike the divided narrative, the united narrative never had a clear spokesperson. However, as I describe in the next section, its central principles can be reconstructed from the practices and observations of prisoners, observers, and staff during the officer strike. In response to divided accounts, radicals foregrounded a particular vision of participatory democracy.[75]

The United Narrative

If we return from the second interpretation of the phrase "the inmates are running the prison" to the first, prisoner self-rule can also be understood as an affirmation of "citizens in a community taking responsibility for changing their own circumstances and achieving their own goals."[76] Members of the NPRA executive board capture this intuition:

> "We want to see Walpole changed so it's compatible with the street, a community prison with self-government, inmate participation and working conditions like on the street," said Robert Dellelo. . . . "We've got to get guards and inmates together and see what we can live with." . . .

> "We don't want to run the prison," said Robert Dussault, . . . NPRA treasurer and a convicted bank robber[.] "We just want a say in how it's run. This is our home."[77]

In other words, the street and the prison occupy the same political and moral space. A community is a community, whether or not its inhabitants are walled in. And every group in a community deserves a say in how it's governed. Moreover, participation in prison life is a kind of political education. "Men who had not gone in as 'political' prisoners," Howard Zinn writes, "who had been what we call common criminals, began emerging rehabilitated. But not in the way the government talks of rehabilitation."[78]

While the particulars of the NPRA's or Zinn's reflections certainly are not representative of all observers or prisoners, the general spirit of their remarks is consistent with an emergent united narrative of the events at Walpole. In this narrative, prisoner self-governance is a form of applied civic education, in which one develops a capacity for complex forms of participation by engaging in more basic participatory acts. At its extreme, this logic points to the possibility that higher-level participation may obviate the need for confinement at all, perhaps even providing a path to prison abolition.[79] At its heart, the united view is an extension of participatory democratic theory to an unfamiliar and unlikely institution: a maximum security prison.

Carole Pateman's classic text *Participation and Democratic Theory* speaks to both the novelty of the united view and its debt to theorists of participatory democracy. Pateman's object of analysis, of course, is the factory, not the prison.[80] Yet Pateman's analysis nicely tracks the vision of self-rule presented by many of the prisoners and observers at Walpole. She writes: "Society can be seen as being composed of various political systems, the structure of authority of which has an important effect on the psychological qualities and attitudes of the individuals who interact within them; thus, for the operation of a democratic polity at a national level, the necessary qualities in individuals can only be developed through the democratization of authority structures in all political systems."[81] Observer descriptions of the consciousness-raising efforts of BANTU, the skills developed in various committees, and the political savvy born of the hum of constant political chatter in the prisoner population all seem to comport with this approach. If one accepts the idea of the prison as a political system (or, in the words of DiIulio, "a constitutional government"), Pateman's advocacy for democracy in industry is in the same genus as the NPRA's call for prisoner self-rule. Furthermore, the similarity between the language used by Pateman and the prisoners and observers at Walpole is striking, perhaps because each tapped into a key piece of the democratic zeitgeist of the late 1960s and early 1970s.

There are limits, however, to setting maximum participation as a lodestar for the democratic reform of punishment. For one, an important lesson from Walpole is that participation is an instrument of management, a tool to achieve various political ends for oneself or for others.[82] Moreover, the observer files underscore that the exclusions potentially remedied by increased participation can be internally complex. Take the negotiated truce between the various factions in the prisoner population as an example. The truce, in essence, morphed the convict code and divisive racial politics into a foundation for a new political order nested within the existing prison order. However, the exhortation to "keep one's house clean" by purging "snitches" and "molesters" suggests that democratic exclusions have a fractal or recursive character.[83] That is, a given exclusion has the quirky feature that it is defined in terms of a simpler, smaller version of itself. Thinking about the pariah class of sex offenders in particular, other works emphasize that communities of sex offenders are also internally divided by status, with those that commit offenses involving children inhabiting the bottom rung. The excluded part of a political order may itself have exclusions that define that part's shape and structure.[84]

The observer files bring into relief another wrinkle for the classic view of participatory democracy. Theorists like Pateman offer a vision of self built on a methodological individualist ontology.[85] It is a world in which the individual is the basic building block of society, a social universe whose atoms are agents with capabilities and preferences.[86] Those working in this register are tempted to write that various forces, whether intentional or accidental, conspired to realize a preexisting capacity for participation within the prisoner population at Walpole. Howard Zinn offers a compelling version of this perspective. However, this view produces two conceptual difficulties.

The first conceptual difficulty is that one cannot posit wards as autonomous agents when it is wards' autonomy, potential or actual, that is called into question in the divided narrative. Extending participatory democratic theory to the prison results in question begging. Put in other words, the central problem is that the individualist, atomic conception of agents precludes investigation into the construction and emergence of the real people and organizations that we reference by the term *agent*.[87] As an alternative, one might treat as fiction the idea that each of us collects and sheds attributes over a lifetime—ambition, depravity, intelligence, charity—while remaining at some base level oneself, one's soul. Custodial institutions, to borrow a phrase from Erving Goffman, are "forcing houses for changing persons," and "each is a natural experiment on what can be done to the self."[88] Treating the "self" in prisoner "self-rule" as an outcome of a tangle of historical and organizational processes rather than as a latent feature of the political world opens up a line of inquiry in which one would otherwise be elided or foreclosed.[89]

The second conceptual tangle, related to the first, concerns the concept of capacity. A key asset of Pateman's view is its holism, its recognition that human abilities are formed intersubjectively and in interaction with one's world. It's clear that the NPRA, for example, would not have been able to govern, and the prisoner population would not have been governable, without a series of previous experiences of collective protest and the tireless consciousness-raising work of outside activists. However, this holism is paired with a tricky assumption that all agents have the *potential* to be full participants in a given decision-making process. This assumption is tricky because in some accounts it entails positing potential as an ahistorical feature of human agency rather than as the product of a historical process.

Consider the following passage from an editorial authored by the committee that ran the observer program: "If we are serious about [rehabilitation], we must develop a new set of expectations, seeing prisoners not as caged, subdued and tamed; but as human beings capable of taking full responsibility for their own lives and their own actions."[90] The appeal to humanity above animality by the Ad Hoc Committee can refer to either an *unbounded* or a *bounded* set of unrealized capabilities. The latter formulation, potential as a bounded set of possible capabilities, is more tenable; potential abilities, like abilities themselves, are constrained by historical context. Take a small example. The ability to work around constraints in prison—the everyday circumvention of restrictions on mail, on distribution of outside material, on the procurement of tools—constitutes a kind of latent political skill. This skill, in turn, can be mobilized toward collective action in a moment of crisis. At Walpole prisoners learned to remove the light fixtures in their cells to jury-rig TV antennas, which enabled them to receive outside news broadcasts during the officer sick-out.[91] More generally, a series of smaller-scale strikes by prisoners within the prison enabled collective learning, producing knowledge about the likely shape and scope of both prisoner and officer response to protest.

DEMOCRATIC FOUNDATIONS

While the events I have examined here are from the 1970s, the contest
over their meaning is contemporary with the politics of our prison reform moment. Advocacies around treatment and control continue to
toe the democratic line of the divided narrative; "[prisoners'] humanity
entitles them to something else: a measure of understanding, and the
mercy that flows from a justice system whose rulers remember that they
too are tempted to do wrong, and often yield to the temptation."[92] Likewise, prisoners' rights and antiprison activists implicitly call upon the
strict egalitarianism of the united narrative; "If we want to do more
than just end mass incarceration—if we want to put an end to the history of racial caste in America—we must lay down our racial bribes,
join hands with people of all colors who are not content to wait for
change to trickle down, and say to those who would stand in our way:
Accept all of us or none."[93] Angela Davis rightly warns that "dangerous
limits have been placed on the very possibility of imagining alternatives.
These ideological limits have to be contested. We have to begin to think
in different ways. Our future is at stake."[94]

What makes the strict egalitarianism of the united view plausible,
alluring even, is that all the parties, and all the capacities, relevant to
a given decision-making process are (or can be) known. As a consequence of this assumption, however, universal inclusion paradoxically
gives rise to a kind of miscount.[95] As the emergence, consolidation,
and disintegration of the prisoners' union at Walpole vividly demon-
strates, there is a gap between the party in a given dispute and the
part of society that party represents. Politics is largely about traversing
this gap, and different parties appear and disappear over the arc of
a given political struggle.[96] By positing a world where *all* individuals
and groups are always already included, the universal egalitarianism
of participatory democracy displaces a discussion of the "mechanisms
of appearance" whereby agents come to be recognized as authors of
political claims.

This challenge reveals an unacknowledged kinship between the united
and divided views. Each attempts to represent and register a world of
difference through narrative; a world of protests, experimental treatment programs, and daily prison violence; and a world of Walpoles that
wriggle and wrench what is meant by the term *democratic participant*.
And each safeguards a particular vision of democracy, of self-government,
by appealing to an intrinsic feature of the political order. For DiIulio, this

intrinsic feature is democratic exclusion; for participatory democrats like Pateman, it's universal inclusion.

At their worst, the divided and united views are not tentative; they know their conclusions before they begin, furtively making their case, blocking objections, and reaching for airtightness. At their best, these views reduce the politics of participation to the resolution of some contradiction or the reenactment of some "deep necessity" of the political order.[97] Such contradictions include that criminals do not have a right to a full schedule of rights or that the capacity for full participation exists *in potentia* for all beings. What's missed in appealing to these supposedly intrinsic features is an openness to novelty in democratic politics.

One of the core claims made by those at Walpole, and a lesson we should heed, was that democracy ought not to be confined to discussions of who should count as a participant, but should be extended to new understandings of what equality means, who possesses it, and where and how it can be practiced.[98] Participation is not a primeval animating force for democratic community but a site-specific accomplishment. And importantly, the meaning of that accomplishment is bound up with the narratives we tell about democracy. Acts as simple as block counts and keeping floors clean can simultaneously be integral to a philosophy of self-rule and to an authoritarian theory of prison management.[99]

The men at Walpole acted knowing that they would likely face severe consequences for their obstinance ("fear of REPRISALS is real"), a prediction that, as Bissonette, Dellelo, and Hamm document in painful detail, proved accurate.[100] At the same time, more subtle forces would come to undermine the NPRA and the more general attempt to formalize the bargaining process between prisoners and prison administrators. In the mid-1970s, state governments like Massachusetts and North Carolina began to decouple prisoners' labor from the corrections budget. That, in addition to the rapidly rising prison population, began to undercut the effectiveness of organized work stoppages and strikes well before the US Supreme Court's decision in *Jones v. North Carolina* in 1977.[101] A reshaping of the political economy of prison labor ultimately narrowed the chances of prisoners to win recognition for their union and implement their alternative, democratic vision of justice.[102]

Labor and the conditions of labor persist as inspiration for prison-based organizing both at Walpole (now MCI-Cedar Junction) and in US prisons more broadly.[103] Water cleanliness and workplace hygiene, for example, motivated a rebellion at MCI-Norfolk and MCI-Cedar Junction in 2017.[104] On a grander scale, more than twenty thousand prisoners across the country engaged in a mass strike over prison labor in 2016, a $2 billion a year industry that employs nearly nine hundred thousand prisoners while paying them a few cents an hour in some states and nothing at all in others. As one incarcerated organizer noted, in an echo of the protestors of a previous generation, "We will not only demand the end to prison slavery, we will end it ourselves by ceasing to be slaves." [105]

CHAPTER 6

Democratic Erosion

The imagination of democratic reformers and the persistence of the question of who governs return us to the questions with which this book began. What are we to make of efforts to democratize custodial institutions? And where do patients and prisoners fit in a democratic political order? This closing chapter contains a few final comments on these questions. I also describe the strengths of my approach and a few weaknesses, then reflect on the normative implications of my analysis.

CUSTODY AND DEMOCRACY

Over the last three chapters we have moved from the wards of St. Elizabeths, to the wider movement for community control, to the cellblocks of Walpole prison. Each case is distant in time—at least a generation—and while each episode takes place in the United States, each involves a different location, culture, and institutional arrangement. The events of Walpole are by all accounts exceptional, the patient government at St. Es more familiar. Confounding matters, in each instance the purpose of custody and the populations in custody appear radically different. Laid before us are snapshots of institutions, seemingly disconnected. What can we possibly learn from such a motley collection of cases? And even if we know more about each episode, do we now know more about the character of the relationship between custody and democracy? I would like to think that we do.

FIGURE 6. Trash fills a cellblock after a rebellion at Walpole State Prison in Walpole, Massachusetts, in 1973. *Source:* Spencer Grant, Boston Public Library.

History is as strange as any fiction. Thinking through complex empirical examples can be an engine for more abstract political theorizing. Throughout this text I have treated the relationship between custody and democracy on three overlapping levels.

On the first level, the smaller and more detailed case studies we've analyzed chip away at a larger, more general understanding of custody. They collectively undermine the authority of what I referred to in chapter 2 as the exclusion thesis. By this term I mean the tendency to think of custodial populations as bounded groups outside the scope of civil society. By confusing empirical limits with conceptual limits, this conviction leaves us with an imagination-constraining misdescription of the political world. As discussed earlier, there is a difference in kind between saying "wards cannot participate," as if we were confronted with a conceptual limit, and the more careful judgment that wards should not participate for contingent, empirical reasons. The former reifies the social prejudices of the day, which by reference to ideal and actually existing alternatives, we ought to question.

On the second level, we have narrative conflict. It's not a straightforward assessment to describe a particular form of organization, custodial or otherwise, as more or less or "democratic." Whether a particular institutional arrangement is recognized as democracy enhancing or detracting is a retrospective judgment that is itself a site of political struggle. Narrative forms and forms of organization are tied together. Nowhere was this on display more vividly, perhaps, than in the debates over community control in custody surveyed in chapter 4.

Messiest of all, the third level of my analysis has been organizational politics itself. The normative project of deepening democratic commitments rests on the possibility of self-government. Throughout this book I've described a tension between democracy *as* therapy and democracy *in* therapy. That means the shaping of ward participation to secure and extend the authority of those already in power in contrast to wards' ability to exert actual influence over the conditions of their care. The product of this tension is a larger ebb and flow: the erosion of custodial authority and the attempt to shore up that authority by canalizing wards' struggles for recognition. Significantly, sometimes custodians' efforts at containment fail. In chapter 5, for instance, prisoners resisted the definition of their situation and attempted to supplant it through an appeal to a different normative order.

What have been the strengths and weaknesses of my approach? Let's start with strengths. On the one hand, my analysis has avoided the weaknesses of a strict constructionist account of competence.[1] I haven't needed to question the underlying reality of the incapacities that in theory justify many custodial relationships in the first place. Competence can be an ontologically objective phenomenon.[2] This makes a discussion of madness, and even childhood (as we saw in chapter 2), a particularly useful companion to criminality.[3] On the other, my account goes further than the standard approach of describing collective action by those in custody as mere remainders, or rounding errors, in an otherwise sufficient theory of democracy. It is a mistake to treat organizations as "dumb pipes," simply channeling information, resources, or skills among their members.[4] We've seen how organizational relationships can make, and remake, wards' competence to make recognizably political claims.

We're left with the rough contours of an overlooked and undertheorized organizational ecology. Custodians and their charges are stuck in what I called in chapter 3 "a strange kind of loop." There is a generative relationship between the organizational processing of ward claims for voice and the democratic processing of the custodial organization itself. Where one might expect to find fixity, totality, and determinism in this loop, we instead see ambiguity and innovation.

The result is not only a remixing of ward self-government but a remixing of repression.[5] Various institutional interests vie to shape ward participation, all while invoking the language and practices of "democratic" management. Repression can achieve its ends through more subtle forms of retrenchment. Working through procedure, wards are disenfranchised through adjustments in who decides, how decisions are made, and where those decisions take place, along with manipulating the incentives for raising claims in the first place. The result is not only the creation of authoritarian spaces but the wider legitimation of those styles of rule.

Let's briefly step back and review each case.

St. Elizabeths. In broad strokes, the case study of Howard Hall describes the institutional mechanisms that made it possible, and made it reasonable, to include patients in ward governance at St. Es in the middle of the twentieth century. The informal, patient-driven innovations that emerged out of Abrahams's original group therapy intervention were institutionalized by the hospital administration. Bolstered by administrative needs (staff shortages, efficiency), intellectual fashion (the rise of psychoanalysis), and psychiatric authorization (deliberation as reality testing), patient self-government groups thrived. The unruly and the unmanageable, the mad, became governable in a new way. Patient speech and action became legible not only to various professions within the hospital but also to fellow patients. While multiplexity made self-government possible, it also, as we saw with the patient federation, created the fault lines that led to its demise.

Community control. An overlooked dimension of the rich, troubled intellectual history of participatory democracy that runs through the 1960s and 1970s is the extension of the idea of community control to prisons and mental hospitals. Those participatory experiments left their mark at both Walpole and St. Elizabeths. In chapter 4 we traced how the goals of "detotalization" and "democratization" structured a number of institutional design choices in this period. Both optimists and pessimists about community control schemes, I suggested, overstated their case. The central weakness of the community control tradition is not this or that organizational design choice, but reformers' tendency to locate both problems, and the solutions to those problems, only in wards themselves.

Walpole. NPRA rule during the Walpole rebellion, I maintained, shouldn't be dismissed as simple mob rule. The glue holding the prison regime together was inmate solidarity. That solidarity was secured by mixing elements of community control, outside social movements, and a central touchstone of prison society: the convict code. While this new prison order had exclusions of its own, along with other wrinkles, it became familiar and legitimate to the men of Walpole. Even after the prison was retaken by prison officers, the truce among prisoner factions persisted for months. When one of the original brokers of that truce escaped from prison, however, Walpole again began to descend into violence. In the final analysis, self-rule was not simply a set of tactics strategically used by prisoners. It became a means to express an alternative, "united" vision of community membership against the conventional "divided" view.

In all, the events described in each case bear directly on questions of care, interest representation, and ultimately, democratic politics. We're left with a description of a domain, or a line of inquiry, and less a collection of fixed results. Custodial organizations are key places where the possibilities of democracy are reimagined, where new democratic subjects are forged, but also places where authoritarian relationships are made and remade.

I've tried to cut my coat according to my cloth. Some will see the scope of my analysis as too provincial to be useful. Still more might argue my claims are too broad, or that they outstrip the evidence I've marshaled. By focusing on edges, on the episodic and the exceptional, my primary ambition has been to unearth anomalies, highlight flawed assumptions, and gesture toward alternatives. The claims I've made here undoubtedly require more empirical investigation to answer questions about their general applicability. I've offered an exploratory analysis, not confirmation.

What's more, over the course of these pages I have likely overemphasized the unity of the broad category of *custody*. As with debates around the category of *disability*, the term is often gerrymandered to serve the interests of particular parties. As I suggested in the first chapter, however, a firm definition both is unnecessary and can actually be counterproductive. One needs only a definition strong enough to assist the machinery of one's theory. A focus on custody avoids cabining potentially informative comparisons of populations that share structurally analogous positions along a number of important dimensions.

On the whole, I believe the strengths of my analysis outweigh its problems. Minimally, it gives a new set of assumptions and premises from which to challenge and rectify the old ones. And at its best it offers a new domain for democratic theory and a set of tools to explore that domain. Throughout the text I have moved, sometimes uneasily, between empirical and normative concerns. In these last few pages I state more clearly what I understand to be the normative stakes of this study.

EROSION

Once we are disabused of the reifications of the exclusion thesis, the next step is less clear. Community control looked to be one plausible alternative to the standard view, but it too appears to be untenable as a general advocacy. Broadly, we've seen that organizational practices do political work on the agents that perform them, often with ambiguous results. Bringing attention to those practices might put us in a better place to make more sensitive normative judgments about how, precisely, custody ought to be organized. Reflection might facilitate deliberation that more reliably secures the implementation of democratic values under the trying circumstances of custody.

One could simply stop here. Unsettling skepticism is a virtue, not a vice; it makes room in deliberation for hard cases, which is a requirement of any viable political theory. Moreover, a general skepticism seems like wise council. It's hard to imagine an alternative course. There is little about novelty, maintenance, or destabilization in organizations that appears "law-like." Routine and regularity, at best, are a function of time and scale.[6] Custodial organizations are no exception. The

PAG in Howard Hall, for instance, could not have emerged even five years earlier.[7] Even if those constraints are overcome, pushing a general technique—say group psychotherapy—or privileging a particular form of custody—perhaps foster care over residential schooling—as more consistent with the ideal of self-government is fraught with difficulties.

However, I want to do a bit more than make a virtue of necessity. I think an affirmative, albeit more speculative, case can be made for publicity as a key backstop against the erosion of custodial relationships.

TWO LESSONS

Surveying the previous chapters, the concern to harmonize democratic politics and custody seems stuck between Scylla and Charybdis. On the one hand we have the errors of the exclusion thesis and on the other the troubled legacy of "democracy in custody." Localism and community control, while containing some promise, have important limits. Chief among those limits, you'll recall, is a tendency to form a boundary around incompetence, to locate its causes and solutions in the people who are experiencing them, and to interpret it in terms that do not require any response or adjustment by those on the outside.

To navigate between these two creatures, we need better bearings. Two lessons from the previous chapters offer a helpful start. One is the importance of treating the disqualifications associated with custody as provisional. The other is that even the best-intentioned custodial designs create opportunities for abuse, exploitation, and repression. Both lessons are two faces of a common threat posed by the use and expansion of custodial relationships: erosion. As I see it, what's required to respond to that threat is an orientation toward custody characterized by humility—and *not* yet another utopian social engineering effort.

Before defending that view, I have a few words on each lesson.

Each case we've examined lends support to the counsel that civic disqualifications should be treated as provisional. Epistemic modesty, and not a pretense to mastery, is better suited to a world in which the line between competent and incompetent is in flux. By provisional, I don't simply mean the straightforward point that a ward might regain a relevant capacity; a mental illness, for instance, that comes and goes over the course of one's life. Nor do I mean that medical or technological innovation might, say, make the addictions or compulsions of some that break the law more amenable to self-management. Yes, those commonsense intuitions, too, support a presumption that disqualification is provisional. Instead, I mean that incompetence is also provisional in that its shape, scope, and structure are defined by the relationship between a given custodial arrangement and the wider account of democracy in which it is embedded.

I'll explain.

For a model of democracy to be complete, it must both define a set of values (such as accountability, liberty, and political equality) and prescribe governance institutions (such as elections, deliberation, and direct participation). Values and institutional practices are typically connected deductively by presuming stylized empirical facts about the psychology and capabilities of individuals and about sociopolitical dynamics.[8] Models, of course, often run afoul of empirical realities. The dynamics of group deliberation, for example, rarely resemble the ideal speech situations imagined by deliberative democrats. If a particular institutional configuration fails to meet an empirical reality, two forms of revision are possible:

The first and more familiar response is to cast about for alternative institutional arrangements that better realize shared democratic values. A second approach is to revise the democratic values themselves in ways that respond to the possibilities and constraints revealed by empirical analysis.[9]

We saw the first kind of revision at St. Elizabeths. The wider institution, and the young psychoanalyst Joseph Abrahams in particular, recognized a misalignment between the purported values of the institution and the organizational mechanisms available and implemented a new method—group therapy—in an attempt to do better. We saw the second form of revision at Walpole. A new organizational form—a mix of the prisoners' union, the peace movement, and the convict code—called into question the traditional, divided narrative of democratic politics. Institutional innovation drove a change in values, not the converse. In both instances, the outcome of the attempt to align values and institutions is better described as a temporary settlement achieved through struggle than as a permanent resolution.

The second lesson is decidedly less optimistic. Each generation appears to discover anew the scandals of incarceration and institutionalization. Each sets out to correct them, and each passes on a legacy of failure. David Rothman writes, "The rallying cries in one period echo dismally into the next. We inherit, in essence, a two-hundred-year history of reform without change."[10] A core line of argument that runs through Rothman's history of asylums and prisons is that when faced with the choice between conscience and convenience, decision-makers routinely chose the latter.

Subsequent scholarship has complicated this story.[11] The decay of reform proposals is not simply a question of choice. *All* organizational forms erode, and the sources of erosion are manifold and usually over-determined.[12] The result is more bleak than traditional worries about social engineering. Those in custody are vulnerable not simply to the ro-manticism of institutional designers but also to the decayed or degraded form of those romantic aspirations. These degraded forms are arguably worse. They lack the coherence of the original plans and, because they are piecemeal, complicate accountability.

Moreover, the consequences of erosion are exacerbated when the form of custody is confinement. As a string of important prison condi-tions cases starting in the 1960s underscores, captive populations are made more vulnerable in virtue of their captivity. The decision to insti-tutionalize or incarcerate leaves wards without recourse to the typical means available on the outside to sustain and defend themselves.[13] Risks are compounded when those in custody do not have the ability, or the tools, to sound the alarm on abuses.

Bringing the two lessons together, an optimism about democratic in-novation and a pessimism about erosion lend support to advocacies that are *antiseptic*—that is, ideals, policies, and institutions that seek to stymie the worst excesses of custodians. Distrust is warranted not be-cause of any particular bad intent but by a clear-eyed assessment of the vulnerability of custodial relationships to the pressures that will inevi-tably be brought to bear upon them. In response, we might draw inspi-ration from older debates over community control during the dawn of the era of mass incarceration. Advocates emphasized the need to bring the actions of custodians before the public for scrutiny and judgment. In doing so, they thought, attention would be drawn to the conditions under which information could be trusted, and to how evaluations of particular custodians, relationships, and institutions might be made in light of that trusted information.[14] The same sentiment, I suspect, is needed now more than ever.

We're rightly horrified by accounts of mistreatment in mental health facilities, overcrowding and violence in prisons, and sexual abuse in detention facilities. However, something is missing by describing these problems simply as a deficit of conditions, of training, or of imagination about institutional design. The intuition generated from the events chronicled in this book is that there is something else at work—not simply the failure of a particular treatment or control regime but a deeper, unresolved democratic deficit. For substantive reforms to occur it is not enough that those who live under intolerable conditions demand change. A wider consensus must be dislodged.[15] Some of the demand must come from those who see the miseries of custody at a distance and decide, finally, enough is enough.

Notes

CHAPTER 1. CUSTODY AND DEMOCRACY

1. David J. Rothman, *The Discovery of the Asylum: Social Order and Disorder in the New Republic* (New York: Aldine Transaction, 2002); Erving Goffman, *Asylums: Essays on the Social Situation of Mental Patients and Other Inmates* (New York: Random House, 1961); Benjamin Reiss, *Theaters of Madness: Insane Asylums and Nineteenth-Century American Culture* (Chicago: University of Chicago Press, 2008); and Thomas L. Dumm, *Democracy and Punishment: Disciplinary Origins of the United States* (Madison: University of Wisconsin Press, 1987).

2. I default to the use of the word *prisoner* instead of *inmate, criminal, convict,* or *incarcerated person.* I do so in the spirit of a long line of advocates who have politicized their status in the prison system. Others, for example, have sought to reclaim the term *convict* (e.g., "convict criminology"). See John Irwin, *The Felon* (Englewood Cliffs, NJ: Prentice-Hall, 1970). Throughout, whatever the term in use, my aim is to use human-first language to describe with dignity the groups that are crudely classified under the label.

3. David J. Rothman, *Conscience and Convenience: The Asylum and Its Alternatives in Progressive America* (New York: Walter de Gruyter, Inc., 2002); and Shai Gortler, "Participatory Panopticon: Thomas Mott Osborne's Prison Democracy," *Constellations: An International Journal of Critical and Democratic Theory* 29, no. 3 (2022): 343–58.

4. Robert Rubenstein and Harold Lasswell, *The Sharing of Power in a Psychiatric Hospital* (New Haven, CT: Yale University Press, 1966).

5. Angela Y. Davis, "Incarcerated Women: Transformative Strategies," *Black Renaissance* 1, no. 1 (1996): 21.

6. Barbara Cruikshank, *The Will to Empower: Democratic Citizens and Other Subjects* (Ithaca, NY: Cornell University Press, 1999).

7. Jonathan Metzl, *The Protest Psychosis: How Schizophrenia Became a Black Disease* (Boston: Beacon Press, 2009); Carol Anderson, *White Rage: The Unspoken Truth of Our Racial Divide* (London: Bloomsbury, 2016); Sarah Staszak, *No Day in Court: Access to Justice and the Politics of Judicial Retrenchment* (New York: Oxford University Press, 2014); and Heather Ann Thompson, *Blood in the Water: The Attica Prison Uprising of 1971 and Its Legacy* (New York: Vintage, 2017).

8. Here I'm following in a venerable tradition of social theorists: Erving Goffman, David Rothman, and Michel Foucault. On "total institutions," see Goffman, *Asylums*.

9. Incapacities are usefully subdivided by their relevance to participation and by their permanence. First, some abilities or disabilities are understood to be largely irrelevant to the capacity to participate, while others are thought to be central. Second, for some groups incapacity is thought to be temporary or curable; for others, incapacity is thought to be a permanent disability. Consider the difference between a young child at an elite boarding school and a patient with late-stage Alzheimer's living out his dotage in hospice care.

10. The term *ward* is used in a similar spirit as I use *custodial institution*. This terminology follows other works that use related terms such as *custodial citizenship*. See Amy Lerman and Vesla Weaver, *Arresting Citizenship: The Democratic Consequences of American Crime Control* (Chicago: University of Chicago Press, 2014).

11. At some point, the facts run out, and we have to make assumptions to move the analysis forward—we have to get our hands dirty. For Harcourt, there is no simple way to choose among approaches: "All rest on different assumptions about human agency and, as a result, are non-falsifiable." As a consequence, we take a leap of faith. We make a kind of ethical choice to get our hands dirty, and we ultimately must pay the price for our decision: "No choice is morally costless." See Bernard E. Harcourt, *Language of the Gun: Youth, Crime, and Public Policy* (Chicago: University of Chicago Press, 2006), 168–74.

12. Gresham M. Sykes, *The Society of Captives: A Study of a Maximum Security Prison* (Princeton, NJ: Princeton University Press, 1958).

13. I see the archive as a kind of disembodied memory; it is "always inflected by the power and authority of those who have colonised the past, whose version of history matter." See Stuart Hall, "Whose Heritage? Un-Settling 'the Heritage', Re-Imagining the Post-Nation," in *The Politics of Heritage*, ed. Jo Littler and Roshi Naidoo (New York: Routledge, 2005), 37–47. On "non-decisions," see Peter Bachrach and Morton Baratz, "Two Faces of Power," *American Political Science Review* 56, no. 4 (1962): 947–52.

14. Some of the figures and activists we'll encounter tried to do more than shift this window. Arguably, their goal was to install an entirely new one.

15. There are a number of ways to elevate the experiences of prisoners and patients. While some focus on first-person narratives, others, like myself, focus on relationships and practices: organizational innovation, adaptation, and ideological challenge.

16. Reiss, *Theaters of Madness*, 17; and Michel Foucault, *Discipline and Punish: The Birth of the Prison* (New York: Vintage Books, 1995).

17. This is not a study about how prisons or hospitals ought to be governed. My purposes are elsewhere. However, for those interested in this topic, there is good work in this vein, for example, David Skarbek, *The Puzzle of Prison Order: Why Life Behind Bars Varies around the World* (New York: Oxford University Press, 2020). To be blunt, I'm not even convinced these institutions, in their past or current forms, should exist at all.

18. In one tradition, we have philosophers eschewing truth claims but drawing their analysis from empirical evidence. Rousseau's conjectural history in the *Discourse on the Origins of Inequality*, for instance, pulled from available travelogues and personal observations about the natural world to fashion a plausible account of the development of human society. In another, we have authors like Robert Dahl who study democracy inductively, by careful examination of the processes that shape political power in a town like New Haven. It's hard to imagine *Polyarchy* being written without the benefit of his careful research in *Who Governs?* A third strand, and the strand closest to my purposes here, highlights the distance between normative claims about democracy and contemporary scientific claims about human behavior. This can be used to throw cold water on existing normative accounts, or it can be used to establish the plausibility of new lines of normative argumentation. Jane Mansbridge does the former with the concept of deliberation and the ideal of the town hall, and Carole Pateman does the latter with her claims about workplace democracy.

19. See John M. Doris, *Lack of Character: Personality and Moral Behavior* (Cambridge: Cambridge University Press, 2002). I am not a historian, as denizens of that camp will quickly recognize. Good historians see understanding the past as its own end. Drawing lessons from that past, or making normative judgments about that past, is at best presentism. For my purposes, however, the history of democratization efforts in custody serves two key "presentist" ends: a source of cautionary tales on the one hand and, on the other, a vehicle to examine the plausibility of wider normative theories of democracy.

20. This is in the spirit of Garfinkel's ethnomethodology: "Ethnomethodological studies analyze everyday activities as members' methods for making those same activities visibly rational and representative for all practical purposes, i.e., 'accountable,' as organizations of commonplace everyday activities." Harold Garfinkel, *Studies in Ethnomethodology* (Cambridge, UK: Polity Press, 1984).

CHAPTER 2. PATIENTS, PRISONERS, CHILDREN, AND TRAVELERS

1. Robert Dahl, *A Preface to Economic Democracy* (Berkeley: University of California Press, 1985). While Dahl leaves this exclusion unexamined in *A Preface to Economic Democracy*, he addresses this "inclusion principle" in more detail in a later work. See Robert Dahl, *Democracy and Its Critics* (New Haven, CT: Yale University Press, 1989).

2. Jane J. Mansbridge, *Beyond Adversary Democracy* (New York: Basic Books, 1980), 237.

3. Benjamin R. Barber, *Strong Democracy: Participatory Politics for a New Age* (Berkeley: University of California Press, 1984), 227–28.

4. Closer to the liberal canon, consider Locke's notes on lunatics in the *Second Treatise*. On the liminal status of the criminal in Locke, see Andrew Dilts, "To Kill a Thief: Punishment, Proportionality, and Criminal Subjectivity in Locke's Second Treatise," *Political Theory* 40, no. 1 (2012): 58–83.

5. By the term *sociality* I simply mean the capacity to live with, and relate to, others in a community. As I note later, whether prisoners can be convincingly included in the same category as children and those with cognitive disabilities is, to a degree, contingent on the philosophy of punishment one embraces.

6. Elizabeth F. Cohen, *Semi-Citizenship in Democratic Politics* (Cambridge: Cambridge University Press, 2009).

7. The terms *competence*, *capacity*, and *qualification* are related, but distinct, in the analysis that follows. By competence I simply mean satisfying a particular threshold among a set of relevant capacities. Often the relevant capacities include rationality, maturity, and sociality. This is not, of course, to say these three are exhaustive. *Qualification* is similar but refers directly to the (often legal) conditions for membership in a particular group or community.

8. Naomi Murakawa and Katherine Beckett, "The Penology of Racial Innocence: The Erasure of Racism in the Study and Practice of Punishment," *Law & Society Review* 44, nos. 3–4 (2010): 695–730; and Bernard E. Harcourt, "Carceral Imaginations," *Carceral Notebooks* 1 (2005): 3–19.

9. I use the terms *mad* and *mad citizen* in the spirit of what Bradley Lewis describes as "mad pride." Among its virtues is that the term reappropriates a disparaging word, emphasizes the historical and scientifically contested status of mental illness and disability, and is inclusive of those who identify as patients, consumers, or survivors. "Rather than pathologizing mental difference, Mad Pride signifies a stance of respect, appreciation, and affirmation." Bradley Lewis, *The Disability Studies Reader*, ed. Lennard Davis (New York: Routledge, 2006), 339. To those that reject this label, my apologies for using it; I hope the book will be considered despite their desire for the use of a different term.

10. Franklin E Zimring, *The Insidious Momentum of American Mass Incarceration* (New York: Oxford University Press, 2020), 184.

11. Martha Nussbaum, *Frontiers of Justice: Disability, Nationality, Species Membership* (Cambridge, MA: Harvard University Press, 2006).

12. Cohen, *Semi-Citizenship in Democratic Politics*.

13. While Ian Shapiro is sharply critical of deliberative theories of democracy, his account of children is largely consistent with deliberative views: "The central challenge of adult-child relations pose for democratic justice is that they are inevitably hierarchical and inegalitarian. But the challenge changes. Children evolve from conditions of utter dependence on adults, to circumstances where equality is possible, to reversed conditions, where once-independent adults become increasingly feeble and dependent sometimes on their adult children, sometimes on others." Ian Shapiro, *Democratic Justice* (New Haven, CT: Yale University Press, 2001), 69.

14. Barber, *Strong Democracy*, 225.

15. Nussbaum, *Frontiers of Justice.*

16. Jennifer Pitts, *Boundaries of the International: Law and Empire* (Cambridge, MA: Harvard University Press, 2018), 77.

17. Dahl, *Democracy and Its Critics,* 3.

18. See generally Charles Taylor, *Dilemmas and Connections: Selected Essays* (Cambridge, MA: Harvard University Press, 2011); Iris Marion Young, *Inclusion and Democracy* (Oxford: Oxford University Press, 2000); and Judith N. Shklar, *American Citizenship: The Quest for Inclusion* (Cambridge, MA: Harvard University Press, 1991).

19. Among other features, a *wicked problem* is one that that is difficult to formulate; is novel; and doesn't admit of a clear, definitive, or uncontroversial solution.

20. As Goodin notes, *exclusion* may not be the best way to couch concerns over democracy. The term is often used euphemistically to refer to issues as varied as participation, citizenship, and migration, to the detriment of analytic clarity. The illusion of thematic unity obscures the fact that different kinds of questions—about entry, about rights, about exit—invite different sorts of arguments Robert E. Goodin, "Inclusion and Exclusion," *European Journal of Sociology* 37, no. 2 (1996): 351.

21. See David Archard, *Children: Rights and Childhood* (New York: Routledge, 2004); Taylor, *Dilemmas and Connections*; and Barber, *Strong Democracy*

22. Eliana Guerra, "Citizenship Knows No Age: Children's Participation in the Governance and Municipal Budget of Barra Mansa, Brazil," *Environment and Urbanization* 14, no. 2 (2002): 71.

23. In Benjamin Barber's participatory approach, for example, the scope of citizenship itself becomes a subject of ongoing discussion and review "and one's participation in such discussion becomes a brief for inclusion." However, to avoid exclusion by the vagaries of power, Barber backs down from rejecting prepolitical foundations entirely. "If the idea of open citizenship is not to become a one-way door through which undesirables are continuously ejected, it must be conditioned by the premise of biological universality." As with Robert Dahl, this premise underscores a need to separate claims about personhood from claims about the proper domain of participatory democratic politics. See Barber, *Strong Democracy*, 227. For a more recent example, see Thomas Christiano, *The Constitution of Equality* (Oxford: Oxford University Press, 2008), 116ff. Others, while more sensitive to the complications disability presents for enfranchisement, draw from a similar set of prepolitical assumptions. See Nussbaum, *Frontiers of Justice*, 331–51.

24. Joel Olson, "Whiteness and the Participation-Inclusion Dilemma," *Political Theory* 30, no. 3 (2002): 389.

25. Olson, "Whiteness and the Participation-Inclusion Dilemma."

26. Arash Abizadeh, "On the Demos and Its Kin: Nationalism, Democracy, and the Boundary Problem," *American Political Science Review* 106, no. 4 (2012): 868–69; and Olson, "Whiteness and the Participation-Inclusion Dilemma."

27. Abizadeh, "On the Demos and Its Kin," 868–69.

28. Christopher Slobogin, *Just Algorithms: Using Science to Reduce Mass Incarceration and Inform a Jurisprudence of Risk* (New York: Cambridge University Press, 2021).

29. Michael J. Cholbi, "A Felon's Right to Vote," *Law and Philosophy* 21, nos. 4–5 (2002): 543–65; and Andrew Dilts, *Punishment and Inclusion* (New York: Fordham University Press, 2014).

30. Barber, *Strong Democracy*, 227. The following quote is from the same source.

31. There is a clear analogy, albeit imperfect, with both Joel Olson's discussion of "Herrenvolk democracy" and what Bernard Harcourt describes as "neoliberal penality." See Olson, "Whiteness and the Participation-Inclusion Dilemma," and Bernard E. Harcourt, *The Illusion of Free Markets: Punishment and the Myth of Natural Order* (Cambridge, MA: Harvard University Press, 2011).

32. Archard, *Children*, 81.

33. John J. DiIulio, *Governing Prisons: A Comparative Study of Correctional Management* (New York: Free Press, 1987), 46.

34. I have in mind Robert Goodin's discussion of special obligations. Robert E. Goodin, "What Is So Special about Our Fellow Countrymen?," *Ethics* 98, no. 4 (1988): 663–86.

35. Shapiro uses the example of children. Sharon Dolovich uses a similar line of argument to describe the situation of prisoners. See her incisive discussion of a society's "carceral burden" in "Cruelty, Prison Conditions, and the Eighth Amendment," *New York University Law Review* 84, no. 4 (2009): 881–979.

36. The right to vote, the right to travel between jurisdictions, and the right to own a gun, for example, can be disaggregated from the more general right of citizenship. In addition, each right—for instance, the right to travel—can itself be disaggregated and graded. See Cohen, *Semi-Citizenship in Democratic Politics*.

37. Ayelet Shachar and Ran Hirschl, "On Citizenship, States, and Markets," *Journal of Political Philosophy* 22, no. 2 (2014): 231–57; and Cohen, *Semi-Citizenship in Democratic Politics*.

38. Frederick G. Whelan, "Prologue: Democratic Theory and the Boundary Problem," *Liberal Democracy* 25 (1983).

39. Ian Shapiro and Casiano Hacker-Cordón, "Outer Edges and Inner Edges," in *Democracy's Edges*, ed. Ian Shapiro (Cambridge: Cambridge University Press, 1999), 1–16.

40. For instance, consider the paradox, described by Bonnie Honig in *Emergency Politics: Paradox, Law, Democracy* (Princeton, NJ: Princeton University Press, 2009), that one needs good people to have good law and good law to make good people. For a review of debates on the democratic boundary problem, see Sarah Song, "The Boundary Problem in Democratic Theory: Why the Demos Should Be Bounded by the State," *International Theory* 4, no. 1 (2012): 39.

41. Robert E. Goodin, "Enfranchising All Affected Interests, and Its Alternatives," *Philosophy & Public Affairs* 35, no. 1 (2007): 40–68.

42. There are a variety of examples one could derive via a reductio ad absurdum. For example, egalitarian decision-making by Hitler's cabinet would, on a

strictly procedural account, make Germany in the late 1930s democratic. See Dahl's rejection of Schumpeterian proceduralism in *Democracy and Its Critics*.

43. Here I have in mind Rousseau's discussion of the injustice of enforcing property law without there having been an initial redistribution of goods among the population.

44. Seyla Benhabib, *The Rights of Others: Aliens, Residents, and Citizens* (Cambridge: Cambridge University Press, 2004), 45.

45. Dahl and, more recently, López-Guerra warn against confusing questions of "membership" with questions about the "unit" of the polity. While the warning is well-taken, my point here is precisely that the two problems share an unacknowledged structural similarity. See Claudio López-Guerra, *Democracy and Disenfranchisement: The Morality of Electoral Exclusions* (New York: Oxford University Press, 2014).

46. Michael Walzer and David Miller, for example. Seyla Benhabib and Arash Abizadeh fit into this latter group.

47. Michael Blake, "Distributive Justice, State Coercion, and Autonomy," *Philosophy & Public Affairs* 30, no. 3 (2001): 257–96.

48. See David Miller, "Why Immigration Controls Are Not Coercive: A Reply to Arash Abizadeh," *Political Theory* 38, no. 1 (2010): 111–20.

49. See Goodin, "Enfranchising All Affected Interests, and Its Alternatives.".

50. David Miller, "Democracy's Domain," *Philosophy & Public Affairs* 37, no. 3 (2009): 228.

51. López-Guerra, *Democracy and Disenfranchisement*.

52. Abizadeh, "On the Demos and Its Kin," 869.

53. Just because one cannot point to the precise moment red becomes blue on the color spectrum, for instance, does not mean that red and blue are the same or that the categories red and blue are incoherent.

54. The distinct period of life we now call *adolescence* can be traced to G. Stanley Hall and the rise of developmental psychology in the early twentieth century. More recently, others have described the emergence of a new category, "youth," that encompasses the period between adolescence and one's midtwenties.

55. For a persuasive discussion, see Jonathan Metzl, *The Protest Psychosis: How Schizophrenia Became a Black Disease* (Boston: Beacon Press, 2009).

56. Most famously, see Michel Foucault's discussion of the delinquent as an organization of "illegalities" in his masterwork *Discipline and Punish: The Birth of the Prison* (New York: Vintage Books, 1995).

57. Compare the class of felonies in 1920 to the class of felonies in 2020. Or, more simply, the number of people impacted by raising or lowering the age of consent.

58. Abizadeh, "On the Demos and Its Kin," 873.

59. I have in mind Andrew Abbott's work on professions, in particular. See Andrew Abbott, *The System of Professions: An Essay on the Division of Expert Labor* (Chicago: University of Chicago Press, 1988). For an illuminating discussion of this point, see Jennifer M. Silva, "Constructing Adulthood in an Age of Uncertainty," *American Sociological Review* 77, no. 4 (2012): 505–22.

60. John Searle, *Making the Social World: The Structure of Human Civilization* (New York.: Oxford University Press, 2010).

61. Gusfield's brilliant study of drunk driving makes this point. Yes, there is a physiological (ontologically objective) reaction to the consumption of alcohol, but the status assigned to drunk driving is a product of collective belief. Joseph R. Gusfield, *The Culture of Public Problems: Drinking-Driving and the Symbolic Order* (Chicago: University of Chicago Press, 1981). This is also why accounts of madness, childhood, and criminality divided along the lines of 'realism' and 'nominalism' create more confusion than clarity.

62. Upshot of David Miller's argument.

63. Upshot of Arash Abizadeh's argument.

64. See Brubaker's discussion of "thinking with trans" and the concept of the "trans of between" in Rogers Brubaker, *Trans: Gender and Race in an Age of Unsettled Identities* (Princeton, NJ: Princeton University Press, 2016).

65. Jo Freeman, "The Tyranny of Structurelessness," *Berkeley Journal of Sociology* 17 (1972): 151–64.

66. López-Guerra, *Democracy and Disenfranchisement*.

67. See Stacy Clifford Simplican, *The Capacity Contract* (Minneapolis: University of Minnesota Press, 2015).

68. Nancy Fraser, "Abnormal Justice," *Critical Inquiry* 34, no. 3 (2008): 393–422.

69. While I reject a subset of candidate interpretations of the exclusion thesis, I leave open the possibility of specifying the conditions necessary for exclusion.

70. This claim is echoed by other social and political theorists. Consider Sewell's discussion of agency and structure: "Structures, I suggest, are not reified categories we can invoke to explain the inevitable shape of social life." William H. Sewell, "A Theory of Structure: Duality, Agency, and Transformation," *American Journal of Sociology* 98, no. 1 (1992): 1–29. Likewise, see Abizadeh's warning that "one must be careful not to redescribe the empirical phenomena in terms of conceptual or metaphysical necessity." Arash Abizadeh, "Does Collective Identity Presuppose an Other? On the Alleged Incoherence of Global Solidarity," *American Political Science Review* 99, no. 1 (2005): 59.

71. This point is indebted to critiques of "political ontology." See Glenn David Mackin, *The Politics of Social Welfare in America* (New York: Cambridge University Press, 2013); Abizadeh, "Does Collective Identity Presuppose an Other?; Patchen Markell, *Bound by Recognition* (Princeton, NJ: Princeton University Press, 2003); and Stephen White, "Weak Ontology and Liberal Political Reflection," *Political Theory* 25, no. 4 (August 1997): 502–23.

72. First-wave feminists like Ernestine Rose fought against coverture, for instance, which was tied to assumptions about a husband's trusteeship over his wife. In subsequent decades, suffragists had to respond to charges that women are child-like and thus unfit to vote. And later movements, to use a more modern example, confronted psychiatric claims of feminine irrationality and disorder.

73. I don't mean to imply all forms of prefigurative politics have this liability. There are various interesting and promising examples, particularly in social movement organizing. See David Graeber, *The Democracy Project: A History, a Crisis, a Movement* (Random House, 2013); and Dean Spade, *Mutual Aid:*

Building Solidarity during This Crisis (and the Next) (London: Verso Books, 2020).

CHAPTER 3. MAD POLITICS

1. Natalie Spingarn, "St. Elizabeths: Pace-Setter for Mental Hospitals," *Harper's Magazine*, January 1956, 63.

2. Goffman appears in the monthly reports of the hospital: "Dr. Erving Goffman has been working in Special Services as a volunteer recreational worker. . . . He has been widely accepted by the personnel and the patients, and seems to be doing his sociology job inconspicuously, as he wished." Jay L. Hoffman to Winfred Overholser, 23 August 1955, Monthly Reports, 1906–1967, Records of the Superintendent (hereafter Monthly Reports), Record Group (hereafter RG) 418, Entry (hereafter E) 22, National Archives and Records Administration (hereafter NARA), Washington, DC.

3. Erving Goffman, *Asylums: Essays on the Social Situation of Mental Patients and Other Inmates* (New York: Random House, 1961), 97.

4. For a discussion of my use of the term *mad*, see chapter 2, note 9. On the use of human-first language, see chapter 1, note 2.

5. That is, basic due process protections for persons subject to indefinite commitment (*O'Connor v. Donaldson*, 422 U.S. 563 (1975)), prisoners who had been transferred to mental hospitals (*Baxtrom v. Herold*, 383 U.S. 107 (1975)), defendants found incompetent to stand trial (*Pate v. Robinson*, 383 U.S. 375 (1966)), and a right to treatment in the least restrictive environment available (*Lake v. Cameron*, 364 F.2d 657 (1966)).

6. While the United States Supreme Court held in 1940 that due process is required in judicial proceedings that involve persons alleged to be mentally ill (*Minnesota v. Probate Court of Ramsey County*, 309 U.S. 270), the contours of that due process right were left ambiguous and largely unenforceable.

7. It was Matthew Gambino's careful archival work in his dissertation on St. Elizabeths that prompted me to start digging for more information on the P.A.C. and Patients' Federation. See Matthew Gambino, "Mental Health and Ideals of Citizenship: Patient Care at St. Elizabeths Hospital in Washington, DC, 1903–1962" (PhD thesis, University of Illinois at Urbana-Champaign, 2010); and Matthew Gambino, "Erving Goffman's Asylums and Institutional Culture in the Mid-Twentieth-Century United States," *Harvard Review of Psychiatry* 21, no. 1 (2013): 52–57.

8. This data, of course, is partial, and inferences made from it need to be carefully contextualized.

9. I redact the patient name with "[patient]" when necessary.

10. "Cover Story," *John Howard Journal* 17, no. 6 (1956): 1 (accessible at St. Elizabeths Hospital Special Collections, Washington, DC; hereafter SEHSC).

11. The administration of St. Elizabeths in the mid-1940s was divided into three clinical branches, each with approximately two thousand patients. Each branch was divided into smaller administrative units called services (Detached Service, Westside Service, Eastside Service, etc.), and each service in turn was composed of one or more buildings, with each building housing a number of

individual wards. Howard Hall housed 170–80 patients in nine wards. "Monthly Journal Is Outlet for the Violently Insane," Monthly Reports, RG 418, E 22, NARA.

12. "Needs of the Hospital," in Annual Report of Saint Elizabeths Hospital for the Fiscal Year 1947, Annual Reports, RG 418, E 20, NARA.

13. "Forbidding and cheerless": see Bernard A. Cruvant, "Maximum Security and the Therapeutic Milieu," *Psychiatric Services* 3, no. 6 (1952): 6–7; "very old": E. D. Griffin to Winfred Overholser, 1 July 1946, Annual Reports, RG 418, E 20, NARA; "obsolete equipment and furnishings": Griffin to Overholser, 1 July 1946, Annual Reports; and "medieval fortress": Joseph Abrahams, interview with author, January 2014.

14. John Tytell, *The Solitary Volcano* (New York: Anchor Doubleday, 1987).

15. Joseph Abrahams, *This Way Out: A Narrative of Therapy with Psychotic and Sexual Offenders* (Lanham, MD: University Press of America, 2010), 1:xiv.

16. Cruvant, "Maximum Security and the Therapeutic Milieu."

17. The glabella is the smooth part of the forehead between the eyebrows. Jerome Kavka to Addison M. Duval, March 1946, Monthly Reports, RG 418, E 22, NARA. A version of this story was also told to me in an interview with Dr. Joseph Abrahams.

18. An editorial in the John Howard Journal describes change of climate in Howard Hall: "In that period prior to the development of any planned therapeutic programs, Howard Hall was feared unit. Patients and personnel both dreaded the words. Some employees even resigned rather than consent to be assigned to work in maximum security. Patients in other units (minimum security) were often told that they would be sent to the Hall if they continue to be uncooperative." [Patient], "Exodus Plus Seven," *John Howard Journal* 18, no. 9 (1966): 6, SEHSC.

19. The escape attempt is described in a monthly report: "General Prisoner [patient] completed his escape by scaling the Howard Hall wall, but General Court-Martial Prison [patient] was apprehended in the outer Howard Hall courtyard and successfully returned to his ward. Rather extensive repairs are being made to the Howard Hall Building to prevent further escapes of this type." Report submitted to Addison M. Duval, April 1946, Monthly Reports, RG 418, E 22, NARA.

20. As Dr. Joseph Abrahams remembers, "Howard Hall had an iron gate, this thing was a medieval castle. It had a reputation as a port of no return. You went to Howard Hall and you were finito." Joseph Abrahams, interview with author, January 2014.

21. Winfred Overholser, foreword to the Annual Report of 1947, Annual Reports, RG 418, E 20, NARA.

22. See generally Gerald N. Grob, *The Mad among Us: A History of the Care of America's Mentally Ill* (New York: Free Press, 1994). To be clear, this was not uniform across all hospitals. Psychosurgery (lobotomies, etc.), for example, never became prominent at St. Elizabeths even when it captured the imagination of mainstream professional psychiatry.

23. On the feasibility of therapy in a large institution, see Goffman's note in *Asylums*, 312.

24. See Gambino, "Mental Health and Ideals of Citizenship," 247. Various other homegrown experiments are evident in the archives, many of which are traced to Dr. Lazelle.

25. For a brief summary of Joseph Abrahams's path to the hospital, see his autobiography, *A Passionate Psychoanalyst.*

26. Martin Summers, *Madness in the City of Magnificent Intentions: A History of Race and Mental Illness in the Nation's Capital* (New York: Oxford University Press, 2019); Michael D'Antonio, *The State Boys Rebellion* (New York: Simon & Schuster, 2004); and Annette Dula, "African American Suspicion of the Healthcare System Is Justified: What Do We Do about It?," *Cambridge Quarterly of Healthcare Ethics* 3, no. 3 (1994): 347–57.

27. Abrahams, *This Way Out,* 1:6.

28. See Abrahams, *This Way Out,* 1:7. "These psychotic people would be engaged in autism, and they would be off in another world. And they're not going to come out of that world unless you're attractive enough in this world. I would talk in an evocative, sometimes provocative manner to lure them." Joseph Abrahams, interview with author, January 2014.

29. Joseph Abrahams, "Preliminary Report of an Experience in the Group Psychotherapy of Schizophrenics," *American Journal of Psychiatry* 104, no. 10 (1948): 613–15.

30. Joseph Abrahams, interview with author, January 2014.

31. In a written commentary on these sessions, Joseph Abrahams notes: "The group met in the day room of Howard Hall 3, in a milieu of 20 patients of various sorts, most of them quiet because of withdrawn schizoid behavior, semi-idiocy, and vegetative general paresis." Abrahams, *This Way Out,* 1:67–68.

32. Procedure and representation were explicitly subjects of discussion. Abrahams writes, "The group went on to discuss organizational matters—seating arrangements, care of property, how to avoid bad feelings over use of books and group property, and the purpose of the group. . . . We discussed parliamentary rules of conduct, and of the possible election of a presiding officer. The group, at my suggestion, decided to elect a member as president for one week at a time, to 'spread it around.'" Abrahams, *This Way Out,* 1:67–68.

33. As an example of the latter, consider the following vignette: "The group began with an election of a new chairman, the problem being brought up by a member who expected to leave the Hall the next day. A number of people were suggested at random by an apathetic group, among who were Foster and Harvey. Harvey ran a strong second to a dark horse candidate. I congratulated the winner, and reminded him that despite the backhand way of the group the position was realized by all to be a responsible one." Joseph Abrahams, *This Way Out: A Narrative of Therapy with Psychotic and Sexual Offenders* (Lanham, MD: University Press of America, 2010), 2:511.

34. Abrahams, *This Way Out,* 1:182.

35. Joseph Abrahams, interview with author, January 2014.

36. Joseph Abrahams to Winfred Overholser, 6 July 1949, Monthly Reports, RG 418, E 22, NARA.

37. Joseph Abrahams to Winfred Overholser, March 1948, Monthly Reports, RG 418, E 22, NARA.

38. Enthusiasm for group therapy appears in various monthly and annual reports; for example: "Group psychotherapy was inaugurated during the past year. This form of therapy is still in the experimental stage but should prove of value as an additional therapeutic procedure in mental hospitals." "Psychiatric Services," in Annual Report of St. Elizabeths Hospital for the Fiscal Year 1947, Annual Reports, RG 418, E 20, NARA.

39. Joseph Abrahams to B. A. Cruvant [margin note], 30 December 1946, Monthly Reports, RG 418, E 22, NARA. Margin notes were a way to express disapproval and, potentially, spell the end of a young intern's or resident's career at St. Elizabeths. One unfortunate resident received the following notation on his file: "Arrogant, egocentric, bombastic, undependable, and uncooperative. Unsatisfactory—BAC."

40. [Patient], "Lost Sheep," *Howard Hall Journal* 1, no. 3 (1948): 2–3, SEHSC.

41. [Patient], "Group Therapy," *Howard Hall Journal* 2, no. 3 (1949): 4, SEHSC.

42. William Hobbs, "Role of Group Psychotherapy in an Admission Service," *Bulletin: A Journal of Group Work at St. Elizabeths Hospital* 5, nos. 1–2 (1961): 4, SEHSC.

43. An anecdote from an interview with Joseph Abrahams, January 2014: "Attendants had repression as primary part of professional identity. Some patients would yell out in the big [integrated] group. Some would go to the john. At one point, the attendants gathered around me, they formed their own group, standing there hostile. 'We can't do this anymore,' 'so and so won't come out of the John.' And I say, 'I don't know about that.' 'We'll take that up in the group.' 'But they're making so much noise!' 'They do get through it, don't they?' 'Yeah.' I then talked to Bernie Cruvant, and said there needs to be a regular training program." Also, from the monthly reports: "Doctor Abrahams has been expanding his work and has given you a good account of some of his problems. One of the chief of these is the Attendant personnel. Just as in the case with physicians, no a large percentage of Attendants are temperamentally qualified to be helpers." Roscoe W. Hall to Winfred Overholser, 30 August 1946, Annual Reports, RG 48, E 20, NARA.

44. Joseph Abrahams describes the unease among hospital staff in an interview: "Usually in mental hospitals the personnel want to keep the patients quiet. Was contentious. The whole point is to keep them quiet. They then learned to talk to each other more normally. Now, there was more noise on the hall, more normal sounds around." He continues, "Some of the attendants at first feared that the leniency would mean greater difficulty in handling the patients and might even provoke rioting." Joseph Abrahams, interview with author, January 2014.

45. Patients mocked this response in an editorial in 1948: "NOW—Webster—says a RIOT is: Wild and loose festivity, revelry, To indulge in an excess of luxury, Create or engage in a disturbance. *Where* and *When* was this Riot that Howard Hall was supposed to have had??????????????????." [Patient], "Bits of This and That," *Howard Hall Journal* 2, no. 3 (1949): 15, SEHSC.

46. Abrahams describes this transformation: "In response to an unspoken evocation on my part, it also began playing a part as a consultative body on

ward problems, which reached its culmination a year later in work with the chief of service, Dr. Bernard Cruvant, when he met with it in what came to be called administrative group therapy." Abrahams, *This Way Out*, 1:11.

47. Over the course of a year, group therapy expanded to include all the Black wards of Howard Hall, then the white wards, then to a larger integrated group.

48. [Patient], "Around the Hall," *Howard Hall Journal* 2, no. 1 (1948): 3, SEHSC.

49. Note, this is eight years before the mandatory desegregation of the hospital in 1954.

50. Abrahams, *This Way Out*, 1:178.

51. "Administrative Group meetings were conducted by the Chief of the Service every other week. These meetings are held in the Howard Hall chapel, which is usually crowded to capacity." William Cushard to Superintendent, 1 July 1954, Annual Reports, RG 418, E 20, NARA.

52. Cruvant, "Maximum Security and the Therapeutic Milieu," 6.

53. Bernard A. Cruvant, "The Function of the Administrative Group in a Mental Hospital Group Therapy Program," *American Journal of Psychiatry* 110, no. 5 (1953): 342–46.

54. [Patient], "Exodus Plus Seven," 6a.

55. Abrahams, *This Way Out*, 2:745.

56. There is, to be sure, a less rosy alternative reading available. Perhaps group therapy, and the presence of psychiatrists in these groups, was meant to facilitate what Erving Goffman called "the mortification of the self." Goffman, *Asylums*. In Goffman's terms, upon entering the institution a patient has a particular "presenting culture" rooted in her home environment. This presenting culture, in turn, comes in conflict with the culture of the institution. The hospital doesn't attempt to achieve a total cultural victory over the patient; rather, it sustains a particular kind of tension between the patient's home world and the institutional world. Over time the patient's self becomes, in steps, "mortified." She is progressively stripped of the support relationships that, prior to entry, constituted her presentation of self. Mortification, Goffman continues, is accompanied by the "reorganization of the self" into the administrative order of the institution. Psychiatric guardianship, in this reading, amounts to overseeing this process.

57. [Patient], "Exodus Plus Seven," 6a.

58. "Peace-time fried chicken": Abrahams, *This Way Out*, 1:xvi; and support for the PAG: [Patient], "Exodus Plus Seven," 6a.

59. [Patient], "Exodus Plus Seven," 6a.

60. Capitalization in the original. [Patient], "Group Therapy," 4.

61. "Patients resisted for a while, then generally complied, though it did interfere with the voluntary nature of those groups." Abrahams, *This Way Out*, 1:xxxii.

62. For example: "The group meeting held on ward 2 last Monday was interesting, despite the fact that we are restricted from talking about paroles and discharges." *An Elizabethan Anthology* (Washington, DC: St. Elizabeths Hospital, 1969), 63, SEHSC.

63. Census of activity groups in 1958 puts the number at approximately eighty-eight. "Approximately," because the groups in the census are combined among "Service and Ward Management Groups, Re-motivational Groups, and Patient Councils." Arnold Peterson, "Report on the Survey of Group Activities," *Bulletin: A Journal of Group Work at St. Elizabeths Hospital* 1, no. 1 (1957), SEHSC.

64. This was similar to how the *Howard Hall Journal* board was elected. See Abrahams, *This Way Out,* 1:293.

65. A small group of patients were deemed too dangerous or as having too severe an illness. You'll see an analogous form of exclusion later in this book at Walpole ("molesters" and "stoolies"). Cushard to Superintendent, 1 July 1954.

66. William Cushard to the Superintendent, 1 July 1955, Annual Reports, RG 418, E 20, NARA.

67. To Winfred Overholser, 9 July 1960, Annual Reports, RG 418, E 20, NARA.

68. "PAC Report," *John Howard Journal* 17, no. 2 (1964): 16, SEHSC.

69. "Cousin Mot," *John Howard Journal* 18, nos. 5–6 (1966): 41, SEHSC.

70. "Speaking Out," *John Howard Journal* 20, no. 10 (1968): 11, SEHSC.

71. Consider this description of the education committee: "A group of six patients have formed a school committee in the hall, and plan on beginning classes in elementary and high school subjects some time during the coming month. We are fortunate in having a patient who has a Master's Degree in education, and who has been placed in charge of the patients' school committee." F. J. Tartaglino to Winfred Overholser, 11 May 1954, Monthly Reports, RG 418, E 22, NARA.

72. William Cushard to Winfred Overholser, 1 July 1954, Annual Reports, RG 418, E 20, NARA.

73. Steven Klinger to the Superintendent, 6 July 1959, Annual Reports, RG 418, E 20, NARA.

74. "PAC Report," 31.

75. Consider the following anecdote: "A committee appointed by the P.A.C. Chairman reported to the Council their proposal. The committee headed by [patient], vice-chairman, submitted their surprising report, which brought strong verbal repugnance from the members of the Council. The committee completely disregarded the purpose for which it was formed, the duty and authority relegated to it by the chair committed the audacious act of completely rejecting the Councils' proposal and substituted one of their own. The Chairman stated, 'The chair doesn't take kindly to the flagrant disregard of purpose. Not only has the committee, without authority, rejected Councils' proposal: it proposes to rob the patients of privileges already granted by the Pavilion visiting regulations.'" "PAC Report," 31.

76. For example: "Dr. Owens frequently becomes annoyed when the chairman of the PAC approaches him to grant the patients privileges, but behind both of their backs groups of men are conniving, disobeying rules and regulations and losing sight of their obligations to their ward community and to themselves." [Patients], "Cooperation," *John Howard Journal* 18, no. 2 (1965): 4, SEHSC.

77. Consider the following: "While all the wards in the Maximum Security Building have certain committees and some degree of self-government, the degree of self-government naturally varies with the type of ward." Klinger to the Superintendent, 6 July 1959.

78. For example: "The work of the executive committee does not merely concern itself obtaining privileges. it is equally the concern of the executive committee and the council to keep what privileges we have obtained. This is done by what is commonly referred to by the staff as EARNED PRIVILEGES. In other words, with each new privilege we acquire there comes a concomitant responsibility." "PAC Report," 16.

79. William Cushard to the Superintendent, 6 December 1956, Monthly Reports, RG 418, E 22, NARA.

80. To David J. Owens, 17 May 1962, Monthly Reports, RG 418, E 22, NARA.

81. This relationship is described in the annual reports of the hospital: "With the marked shortage of employee help in the hospital, the patients themselves have done much in helping to control difficult situations on the wards. Many times an employee might have been hurt if not for the intervention of patients." Francis J. Tartaglino to Winfred Overholser, 15 July 1957, Annual Reports, RG 418, E 20, NARA.

82. David Harris to Francis Tartaglino, 6 August 1956, Monthly Reports, RG 418, E 22, NARA.

83. For example: "Efforts have been made by the hospital to obtain pay raises for both the residents and the staff physicians but no action has been taken on these recommendations. The staff shortage of physicians continues. I feel this is due primarily to the low salary scale and the lack of fringe benefits." Evelyn B. Reichenbach to Winfred Overholser, 4 August 1959, Annual Reports, RG 418, E 20, NARA.

84. Consider the following: "The patients [on Pine ward] now have an administrative group and a group therapy session.... Complaints have since disappeared and the patients now seem quite content." Tartaglino to Overholser, 15 July 1957.

85. David Harris to Winfred Overholser, 8 May 1962, Monthly Reports, RG 418, E 22, NARA.

86. A supervisor on the William A. White Service explains that "rehabilitation and discharge of the patients from the hospital is the goal of our treatment program. If this cannot be accomplished the aim should to help the patient become a useful hospital citizen."

87. This commotion is described in various editorials in the patient newspaper; for instance: "Dec 1965, The Editorial for last month ... caused quite a stir in John Howard. It also had a few unpleasant side effects—it stirred the emotions and excited them to verbal outbursts.... [C]ries of 'Who does he think he is?' were heard everywhere." [Patient], "The Christmas Season—A Time for Harmony," *John Howard Journal* 17, no. 12 (1965): 5, SEHSC; and [Patient], "Editorials," *John Howard Journal* 17, no. 11 (1965): 5, SEHSC.

88. Unbracketed ellipses are in the original. [Patient], "Together or Apart—The Choice Is Your[s]," *John Howard Journal* 17, no. 12 (1965): 20, SEHSC.

89. After this issue, and in the wake of decreasing patient support for the *John Howard Journal*, there was a two-month publication hiatus.

90. William Cushard to the Superintendent, 2 July 1956, Annual Reports, RG 418, E 20, NARA.

91. Dix does not include Howard Hall; it contains patients with more general grounds privileges. "Plans are also being made to organize a self-government group on Cedar and Spruce Wards. This group has already had its first meeting and has elected its Chairman, and Committees have been formed." F. J. Tartaglino to Winfred Overholser, 9 July 1955, Annual Reports, RG 418, E 20, NARA.

92. For example: "There was a complete absence of ward activity. No occupational therapy, group therapy, or similar activities were available. Unlike the other wards in Dix, there was no self-government. . . . Patients themselves appeared apathetic, sitting around in chairs staring at the four walls, seemed to be invested in little or nothing, and seemed unable to become integrated in any type of relationship. . . . As a result a concerted effort was evolved, personnel was changed, and dedicated and invested personnel were transferred to the ward. The following operations were initiated: A ward group was begun. Patients through the medium of this group formed a self-government, they initiated an occupational therapy of their own for which patients on the ward took the responsibility, as the O.T. workers' time was already fully occupied on the other wards. . . . Within a period of three weeks the following changes in the ward were noted: Patients appeared much more vivacious, showed a considerable investment in each other and in the ward in general. . . . Perhaps the most outstanding change is the well-defined esprit de corps that has evolved in this short period of time. In fact, recently we have been able to leave the ward door unlocked." A. H. Kiracofe to David Harris, 30 April 1957, Monthly Reports, RG 418, E 22, NARA.

93. In August 1956, "the patients' congress is developing, and during the month they presented me with a most thoughtful, practical plan for patient operation of the elevators to relieve hospital personnel. I endorsed the plan and have forwarded it through channels." Harris to Tartaglino, 6 August 1956.

94. Consider the following: "Patients' congress activity of the month was a large party in the patio." Joseph Abrahams to Winfred Overholser, 22 July 1954, Annual Reports, RG 418, E 20, NARA. There is also a nice anecdote about going out to see flowers. David Harris to Manson Pettit, 6 April 1959, Monthly Reports, RG 418, E 22, NARA.

95. See To the Superintendent, 5 July 1957, Annual Reports, RG 418, E 20, NARA: "The administrative groups on open wards have been quite effective in obtaining the patients' cooperation on the basis of their self-respect. Their efforts make it possible for the Service to function with a shortage of personnel, though there are many instances in which the need for personnel supervision is clearly demonstrated for therapeutic value."

96. To Winfred Overholser, 30 July 1958, Annual Reports, RG 418, E 20, NARA.

97. For example: "As a result a concerted effort was evolved, personnel was changed, and dedicated and invested personnel were transferred to the ward." Kiracofe to Harris, 30 April 1957.

98. David Harris to Francis Tartaglino, 6 March 1957, Monthly Reports, RG 418, E 22, NARA.

99. David Harris to Francis Tartaglino, 3 June 1957, Monthly Reports, RG 418, E 22, NARA.

100. For an example of this enthusiasm, consider the fowllowing: "In Dix, however, the residents participate much more intensively in administrative matters affecting the patients on their wards. The problems which are raised by patients are handled individually, based on the merits of the particular problem. In order for this system to operate effectively, it is necessary for the doctor to know his patients intimately and extensively; otherwise he is unable to make the decisions or recommendations called for." Jay Hoffman to Winfred Overholser, 27 November 1956, Monthly Reports, RG 418, E 22, NARA.

101. See Gambino's excellent dissertation on this point: "Nevertheless, in February of 1957, Overholser abruptly banned mixed-race dancing at the hospital. The immediate impetus appears to have involved illicit sexual contact between patients. Officials had always worked to minimize 'inappropriate petting' at dances, but the prospect that such contact might occur openly between black male and white female patients may have finally prompted them to administrative action." Gambino, "Mental Health and Ideals of Citizenship," 201. David Harris to Francis Tartaglino, 5 April 1957, Monthly Reports, RG 418, E 22, NARA. In the margins of the report: "[N]o solution! WO [Winfred Overholser]."

102. Administrators describe the formation of the federation here: "The Patients' Federation had its first meeting at two p.m. on April 2nd, as a result of the proposal initiated by the patients' congress of this [Dix] service. I think it will be a useful organization, and we are currently continuing to work out some of the birth problems." Harris to Tartaglino, 5 April 1957.

103. Anne Bushart to the Superintendent, October 1958, Monthly Reports, RG 418, E 22, NARA.

104. Harris to Tartaglino, 5 April 1957.

105. Quoted in Gambino, "Mental Health and Ideals of Citizenship," 272.

106. Approval of the federation is mentioned in the monthly reports of the hospital: "There are a number of administrative details that need yet to be worked out in regard to this project. Many of the nurses, and at least one of the Clinical Directors, have been unwilling to have their patients participate in the "Patients' Federation" without clear and written indication that the Superintendent approves of this project. A draft memorandum will be submitted to the Superintendent shortly regarding this matter. [Pen notes in margin:] Done. WO [Winfred Overholser]." Jay Hoffman to Winfred Overholser, 24 April 1957; Monthly Reports, RG 418, E 22, NARA.

107. The basic structure is described here: "Some twenty-five meetings go on monthly (almost one daily). These involve a group of patients ranging from ten to fifty in number, which meets with one doctor, nurse, social worker, aide or attendant and practical matters of ward and service management are discussed, as well as behavior of patients. Often the interactions get into the areas of personal problems. These meetings go on at the ward level (ward councils), and representatives from these form the executive council. Representatives from the latter attend the Patients' Federation." To the Superintendent, 1 July 1957.

108. Anne Bushart to the Superintendent, July 1958, Monthly Reports, RG 418, E 22, NARA.

109. To the Superintendent, 11 July 1958, Monthly Reports, RG 418, E 22, NARA.

110. To the Superintendent, 5 July 1957.

111. Quoted in Gambino, "Mental Health and Ideals of Citizenship," 273.

112. "St. Elizabeths Hospital," in *Annual Report of the U.S. Department of Health, Education, and Welfare* (1957): 3, SEHSC. In the record, however, it's referred to as a congress, not a federation.

113. Evelyn B. Reichenbach to Winfred Overholser, 30 July 1958, Annual Reports, RG 418, E 20, NARA; and Reichenbach to Overholser, 4 August 1959.

114. To the Superintendent, 5 July 1957.

115. Put in other terms: a particular organizational form, while not initially having the full support and participation of the patient population, might mobilize interest, improve legitimacy, and in turn generate further cycles of (democratic) organizational innovation.

116. Anne K. Bushart to Winfred Overholser, October 1958, Monthly Reports, RG 418, E 22, NARA.

117. It moved from the basement of one of the halls to the Red Cross (recreation) building. Anne K. Bushart to Winfred Overholser, November 1957, Monthly Report, RG 418, E 22, NARA.

118. Anne K. Bushart to Winfred Overholser, May 1958, Monthly Reports, RG 418, E 22, NARA.

119. Mason B. Pettit to Winfred Overholser, 14 July 1959, Annual Reports, RG 418, E 20, NARA.

120. For an overview, see Alisa Roth, *Insane: America's Criminal Treatment of Mental Illness* (New York: Basic Books, 2018), 88ff.

121. Jay Hoffman to Winfred Overholser, 9 November 1954, Monthly Reports, RG 418, E 22, NARA.

122. To Winfred Overholser, 30 July 1958, Monthly Reports, RG 418, E 22, NARA.

123. Annual reports in 1959 reflect a general change in attitude toward the federation; for example: "I believe that during the year things have "tightened up" a bit perhaps constructively in our attitude towards our privileged patients." Manson B. Pettit to Winfred Overholser, 14 July 1959, Annual Reports, RG 418, E 20, NARA. "The Patients' Congress continues to influence treatment in a modest fashion through the maintenance of an organized patient enthusiasm." David Harris to the Superintendent, 7 July 1959, Annual Reports, RG 418, E 20, NARA. In addition, "the Patients' Federation no longer functions as it was a complete failure and led to many complications. It is hoped within the next year that this group can be re-established because, in my opinion, it may serve a very useful function if properly directed." Reichenbach to Overholser, 4 August 1959.

124. [Patient], "Together or Apart," 19.

125. This is not to say that they were "ungoverned" before, but simply that a new technique of government came into being.

126. The preceding narrative is a resource for theorizing in much of the same way "ordinary language" is a resource for textual interpretation and philosophical exploration. It shows how, and why, certain ordinary concepts, from guardianship to representation, feel familiar or strange in a given context. The identification of aberration is crucial, for it helps us to "be brutal with, to torture, to fake and to override, ordinary language" and intuitions. John L. Austin, "A Plea for Excuses: The Presidential Address," *Proceedings of the Aristotelian Society* 57 (1956): 186. By putting concepts "under pressure, brutality of this kind exposes the substructure of norms and metaphors that permit, prevent, or (in some cases) require certain ways of using language." Colin Bird, "Political Theory and Ordinary Language: A Road Not Taken," *Polity* 43, no. 1 (2011): 111.

127. Judi Chamberlin, *On Our Own: Patient-Controlled Alternatives to the Mental Health System* (New York: McGraw-Hill, 1978), 16.

128. While granting that what "schizophrenics" say in groups has meaning, that meaning, Laing claimed, only emerged through translation.

129. Chamberlin, *On Our Own*, xiii.

130. See William H. Sewell, "A Theory of Structure: Duality, Agency, and Transformation," *American Journal of Sociology* 98, no. 1 (1992): 1–29. Structures are both the medium and outcome of social relations.

131. The mechanics of this basic relationship are elegantly articulated by Reiss, who describes the relationship between patient culture and the institution as "dialectical." The loop that I describe is a direct extension of his discussion in Benjamin Reiss, *Theaters of Madness: Insane Asylums and Nineteenth-Century American Culture* (Chicago: University of Chicago Press, 2008).

132. We've seen that this is as true for custodial care of the mad as it is, for instance, for welfare state policies generally. On participation and the welfare state, see Joe Soss, *Unwanted Claims: The Politics of Participation in the Us Welfare System* (Ann Arbor: University of Michigan Press, 2002).

133. In their study of the Yale Psychiatric Institute (YPI) in the 1960s, Rubenstein and Lasswell describe an "authoritarian hospital" at which "society and the doctors, experts with extraordinary authority over the lives of others, justify such exemptions from democratic practices and drastic usurpation of rights by describing those with mental illnesses as fragile, childlike, irresponsible, and dangerous to themselves and others." Robert Rubenstein and Harold Lasswell, *The Sharing of Power in a Psychiatric Hospital* (New Haven, CT: Yale University Press, 1966), 5. While Lasswell's "policy science of democracy" has largely fallen into disrepute (e.g., Laurence H. Tribe, "Policy Science: Analysis or Ideology?," *Philosophy & Public Affairs* 2, no. 1 (1972): 66–110; and John S. Dryzek, "Policy Sciences of Democracy," *Polity* 22, no. 1 (1989): 97–118), the tension between power sharing and treatment diagnosed at YPI persists in the contemporary discussions of mental health care. Joel Tupper Braslow, "The Manufacture of Recovery," *Annual Review of Clinical Psychology* 9 (2013): 781–809.

134. They're a large percentage of state prison populations, more likely to be victimized within prison, overrepresented in instances of use of force within

prison walls, overrepresented in use of administrative segregation, and disproportionately represented among probationers and parolees. See generally Bruce B. Way et al., "Characteristics of Inmates Who Received a Diagnosis of Serious Mental Illness upon Entry to New York State Prison," *Psychiatric Services* 59, no. 11 (2008): 1335–37. An increasingly wide body of scholarship underscores the interaction of madness and criminalization: in gun-control policy, in trying juveniles as adults, in mass incarceration, and in prisoner reentry policy, to name a few examples. e.g., Jonathan M. Metzl and Kenneth T. MacLeish, "Mental Illness, Mass Shootings, and the Politics of American Firearms," *American Journal of Public Health* 105, no. 2 (2015): 240; Bernard E. Harcourt, *The Illusion of Free Markets: Punishment and the Myth of Natural Order* (Cambridge, MA: Harvard University Press, 2011); Michael Rembis, "The New Asylums: Madness and Mass Incarceration in the Neoliberal Era," in *Disability Incarcerated: Imprisonment and Disability in the United States and Canada*, ed. Liat Ben-Moshe, Chris Chapman, and Allison C. Carey (New York: Palgrave Macmillan, 2014), 139–59; and Liat Ben-Moshe, Chris Chapman, and Allison C. Carey, eds., *Disability Incarcerated: Imprisonment and Disability in the United States and Canada* (New York: Palgrave Macmillan, 2014). Even a cursory reading of this literature leaves one with an image of modern democratic citizenship as embedded within, and dependent upon, a medicalized, psychiatrized, and ultimately punitive discourse of madness.

135. The struggle is both epistemic and political. "The very heart of [mad activism] begins with expressly biomedical assignments of impairment. This comes not in the form of a general pronouncement of inferiority, but in a direct and specific diagnosis and treatment process. Because of this, Mad Pride and disability activist efforts to reduce individualization, medicalization, and ableism require a dual struggle that goes beyond politics-as-usual." Bradley Lewis, "A Mad Fight: Psychiatry and Disability Activism," in *The Disability Studies Reader* (New York: Routledge, 2006).

136. Reiss, *Theaters of Madness*.

137. Reiss, *Theaters of Madness*, 197.

CHAPTER 4. COMMUNITY CONTROL IN CUSTODY

1. Much of the historical record, newspaper coverage, and general commentary refers to this episode—and others like it—as "riots," "unrest," and "collective disorder." This language often obscures more than it reveals. Instead, when appropriate, I opt to use terms such as *strike, stoppage, revolt, rebellion,* and *protest* to emphasize the political significance of these events. Hinton, for example, justifies her use of "rebellion" in a similar manner: "The so-called urban riots from the 1960s to the present can only be properly understood as *rebellions.* These events did not represent a wave of criminality, but a sustained insurgency." See Elizabeth Hinton, *America on Fire: The Untold History of Police Violence and Black Rebellion Since the 1960s* (New York: Liveright Publishing, 2021), 7. Heather Ann Thompson makes a related point about the Attica "uprising" in *Blood in the Water: The Attica Prison Uprising of 1971 and Its Legacy* (New York: Vintage, 2017).

2. Tom Murton and Joe Hyams, *Accomplices to the Crime* (New York: Grove Press, 1969); J. E. Baker, *Prisoner Participation in Prison Power* (Metuchen, NJ: Scarecrow Press, 1985); John Irwin, *Prisons in Turmoil* (Boston: Little, Brown, 1980); and James Jacobs, *Stateville: The Penitentiary in Mass Society* (Chicago: University of Chicago Press, 1977), 205.

3. Baker, *Prisoner Participation in Prison Power*, 71.

4. See generally Jeffrey Hardy, *The Gulag after Stalin* (Ithaca, NY: Cornell University Press, 2016).

5. J. E. Baker, *The Right to Participate: Inmate Involvement in Prison Administration* (Metuchen, NJ: Scarecrow Press, 1974); Baker, *Prisoner Participation in Prison Power*; Murton and Hyams, *Accomplices to the Crime*; Irwin, *Prisons in Turmoil*; John Irwin, *The Felon* (Englewood Cliffs, NJ: Prentice-Hall, Inc., 1970); and Angela Yvonne Davis, *Are Prisons Obsolete?* (New York: Seven Stories Press, 2003).

6. Participatory management in custody is at least as old as the birth of the modern penitentiary. The trusty system, for example, has a violent and troubled history. Warden Thomas Murton, tasked with responding to crisis in the Arkansas prison system in the late 1960s, notes: "According to Arkansas logic, men convicted of violent acts were just the ones to be given weapons under such a brutal system, because they had already demonstrated their willingness to assault others." See Murton and Hyams, *Accomplices to the Crime*, 25. Moreover, prisoner participation did not go unnoticed by more well-meaning reformers, who tried to bend prisoner involvement to particular penological purposes. Among the most famous in the last century, for example, was Howard Gill at the Norfolk State Prison Colony in the late 1920s. He viewed the facility as a "shared community" without bars. The prison was organized around cottage-like dormitories and even included a debating society. Similarly, Thomas Osborne's "mutual welfare league" at Auburn, Zebulon Brockway's system of parole at Elmira, and LaMar Empey's Provo and Silverlake "peer-group" experiments all embraced personal reformation through guided practices of self-government.

7. Alan Altshuler, *Community Control: The Black Demand for Participation* (New York: Pegasus Press, 1970).

8. Daniel P. Moynihan, *Maximum Feasible Misunderstanding* (New York: Free Press, 1969). See generally the work of Bernard Harcourt, Loïc Wacquant, and Naomi Murakawa. They see the modern carceral state as the culmination of a distinctly *liberal* law and order politics. See Naomi Murakawa, *The First Civil Right: How Liberals Built Prison America* (New York: Oxford University Press, 2014).

9. Altshuler, *Community Control*, 144.

10. The principle of decentralization was built from three smaller conceptual components. The first concerns scale. The scale of government should not be so small as to be ineffective, but also should not be so large as to disconnect citizens from their representatives. I call this the concept of *local autonomy*. Second, even if local authoritie, fos arer example, less competent than officials at a higher level, responsiveness to local preferences—up to a point—ought to be prioritized. I call this second component the concept of *local taste*. The general

prejudice against the competence of community members, advocates suggested, is, in part, truth. Simply distributing resources to neighborhoods to combat poverty, illness, and violence is important but not enough. Collective incompetence, advocates argued, is the result of both oppression and paternalism. Removing a group from the experience of self-government simply entrenches its powerlessness. Involving members of the community should make the neighborhood conscious of the problems of delinquency, collectively interested in the welfare of its own, and active in promoting programs for improvements in the community environment. I call this third element of decentralization the concept of *local competence*. See Ernest W. Burgess, Joseph D. Lohman, and Clifford R. Shaw, "The Chicago Area Project," in *Coping with Crime*, ed. Marjorie Bell (New York: Yearbook of the National Probation and Parole Association, 1937), 8–28.

11. Donald Clemmer, *The Prison Community* (Boston: Christopher Publishing House, 1940).

12. Charles Stastny and Gabrielle Tyrnauer, *Who Rules the Joint? The Changing Political Culture of Maximum-Security Prisons in America* (Lexington, KY: Lexington Books, 1982), 33–34.

13. Baker, *Prisoner Participation in Prison Power*, 56.

14. Kitty Calavita and Valerie Jenness, *Appealing to Justice: Prisoner Grievances, Rights, and Carceral Logic* (Oakland: University of California Press, 2014).

15. Baker, *Prisoner Participation in Prison Power*, 64.

16. David D. Dillingham and Linda R. Singer, *Complaint Procedures in Prisons and Jails: An Examination of Recent Experience* (Washington, DC: US Department of Justice, National Institute of Corrections, 1980), 14.

17. Baker, *Prisoner Participation in Prison Power*, 184.

18. Baker, *Prisoner Participation in Prison Power*, 65.

19. Baker, *Prisoner Participation in Prison Power*, 71.

20. Vesla Weaver and Amy Lerman, "A Trade-Off between Safety and Democracy? An Empirical Investigation of Prison Violence and Inmate Self-Governance," in *Democratic Theory and Mass Incarceration*, ed. Albert W. Dzur, Ian Loader, and Richard Sparks (Oxford: Oxford University Press, 2016), 241.

21. Baker, *Prisoner Participation in Prison Power*, 71.

22. Cited in Stastny and Tyrnauer, *Who Rules the Joint?*, 92.

23. This figure is from Dillingham and Singer, *Complaint Procedures in Prisons and Jails*, 21. However, there is some controversy over these numbers; see Baker, *Prisoner Participation in Prison Power*, 71.

24. Donald Tibbs, *From Black Power to Prison Power: The Making of Jones v. North Carolina* (New York: Palgrave, 2012), 112.

25. Irwin, *Prisons in Turmoil*.

26. Tibbs, *From Black Power to Prison Power*, 137.

27. For example, Stastny and Tyrnauer, *Who Rules the Joint?*

28. For example, *Attica: The Official Report of the New York State Special Commission on Attica* (New York: Bantam Books, 1972).

29. For example, Baker, *Prisoner Participation in Prison Power*.

30. Irwin, *Prisons in Turmoil*.

31. For example, Jamie Bissonette, *When the Prisoners Ran Walpole: A True Story in the Movement for Prison Abolition* (Cambridge, MA: South End Press, 2008).

32. Jacobs, *Stateville*.

33. Jacobs, *Stateville*, 208–9; and John J. DiIulio, *Governing Prisons: A Comparative Study of Correctional Management* (New York: Free Press, 1987).

34. David Skarbek, "Governance and Prison Gangs," *American Political Science Review* 105, no. 4 (2011): 702–16.

35. Jonathan Simon, *Mass Incarceration on Trial: A Remarkable Court Decision and the Future of Prisons in America* (New York: New Press, 2014).

36. Marie Gottschalk, *The Prison and the Gallows: The Politics of Mass Incarceration in America* (New York: Cambridge University Press, 2006); Murakawa, *First Civil Right*; and Marie Gottschalk, *Caught: The Prison State and the Lockdown of American Politics* (Princeton, NJ: Princeton University Press, 2015).

37. Noel A. Cazenave, *Impossible Democracy: The Unlikely Success of the War on Poverty Community Action Programs* (Albany: State University of New York Press, 2007); Elizabeth Hinton, *From the War on Poverty to the War on Crime* (Cambridge, MA: Harvard University Press, 2016); Robert Halpern, *Rebuilding the Inner City: A History of Neighborhood Initiatives to Address Poverty in the United States* (New York: Columbia University Press, 1995); and Dan Berger and Toussaint Losier, *Rethinking the American Prison Movement* (New York: Routledge, 2017).

38. I'll mention a few examples. Advocates of restorative justice see lawbreakers as a part of, not outside, the relevant community of interest for prison reform. Techniques like "circles" are intended to embody an inclusive community of care. As John Braithwaite argues, community incapacitation is more inclusive, and less clumsy, than its carceral incapacitation counterpart. John Braithwaite, *Restorative Justice & Responsive Regulation*, Studies in Crime and Public Policy (Oxford: Oxford University Press, 2002). More recently, a number of legal scholars have come together under the banner of "democratizing criminal law." Laura I. Kleinfeld, Joshua Appleman, and Thomas F. Geraghty, "White Paper of Democratic Criminal Justice," *Northwestern University Law Review* 111 (2016): 1693. They argue a persistent barrier to reform is that bureaucratic attitudes are divorced from the public's attitudes and sense of justice; consequently, the solution is to make criminal justice more community focused and responsive to lay interests. See also Albert Dzur, "Participatory Democracy and Criminal Justice," *Criminal Law and Philosophy* 6, no. 2 (2012): 115–29.

As a further example, in the Movement for Black Lives platform, organizers demand "a world where those most impacted in our communities control the laws, institutions, and policies that are meant to serve us—from our schools to our local budgets, economies, police departments, and our land—while recognizing that the rights and histories of our Indigenous family must also be respected." Here, the justification is more normative than instrumental. Invoking a version of the "all-affected interests" principle (Robert E. Goodin, in "Enfranchising All Affected Interests, and Its Alternatives," *Philosophy & Public Affairs* 35, no. 1 [2007]: 40–68), advocates claim that community control in policing, among other criminal justice domains, corrects not only defects of policy but democratic misrepresentation. See "A Vision for Black Lives: Policy Demands for Black Power, Freedom, and Justice," The Movement for Black Lives, April 18, 2018, https://policy.m4bl.org/community-control/.

39. DiIulio, *Governing Prisons*, 47.

40. DiIulio, *Governing Prisons*, 38.

41. Weaver and Lerman, "Trade-Off between Safety and Democracy?," 250.

42. I have in mind the work of Archon Fung and his collaborators. See also Albert Dzur, *Democracy Inside: Participatory Innovation in Unlikely Places* (New York: Oxford University Press, 2019).

43. David Skarbek, *The Puzzle of Prison Order: Why Life Behind Bars Varies around the World* (New York: Oxford University Press, 2020).

44. Ann Chih Lin, *Reform in the Making: The Implementation of Social Policy in Prison* (Princeton, NJ: Princeton University Press, 2000).

45. Jacobs, *Stateville*.

46. Stastny and Tyrnauer note: "Historically prison-reform experiments have been made through the leadership and nurturing of reform wardens, Osborne and Gill among them. When support at the system's center was withdrawn, their projects could not survive." Stastny and Tyrnauer, *Who Rules the Joint?*, 180.

47. Nicola Lacey, *The Prisoners' Dilemma* (Cambridge: Cambridge University Press, 2008).

48. Christopher D. Berk, "Must Penal Law Be Insulated from Public Influence?," *Law and Philosophy* 40, no. 1 (2021): 67–87.

49. Dzur, "Participatory Democracy and Criminal Justice."

50. Elizabeth Hinton, for example, has argued for turning prisons into community colleges. Elizabeth Hinton, "Turn Prisons into Colleges," *New York Times*, March 6, 2018.

51. Angela Y. Davis, "Incarcerated Women: Transformative Strategies," *Black Renaissance* 1, no. 1 (1996): 21.

52. See Davis, *Are Prisons Obsolete?*

53. Antony Duff, *Punishment, Communication, and Community* (New York: Oxford University Press, 2001), 30–31.

54. Barbara Cruikshank, *The Will to Empower: Democratic Citizens and Other Subjects* (Ithaca, NY: Cornell University Press, 1999); and Glenn Mackin, "Inventing Democratic Subjectivity in the 1960s Community Action Programs," *New Political Science* 42, no. 1 (2020): 52–69.

55. Carole Pateman, *Participation and Democratic Theory* (Cambridge: Cambridge University Press, 1970).

56. More generally, it's a mistake to treat the prison as a self-enclosed social system; the "community" in custodial community control doesn't stop at the prison entrance. For example, Megan Comfort, *Doing Time Together: Love and Family in the Shadow of the Prison* (Chicago: University of Chicago Press, 2008).

57. Samuel Cutler, "Prisoners at Norfolk Reassured by Doyle," *Boston Globe*, March 2, 1946, 1.

58. Malcolm X, *The Autobiography of Malcolm X (as Told to Alex Haley)* (New York: Random House, 1965).

59. J. E. Baker, *The Right to Participate: Inmate Involvement in Prison Administration* (Metuchen, NJ: Scarecrow Press, 1974).

60. Gresham M. Sykes, *The Society of Captives: A Study of a Maximum Security Prison* (Princeton, NJ: Princeton University Press, 1958).

61. "Grossman Listens for Hour in Prison to Convicts' Demands," *Boston Globe*, July 23, 1952, 14.

62. Baker, *Right to Participate*, 32.

63. "The Siege of Cherry Hill," *Time Magazine*, January 31, 1955, 17.

64. Bissonnette, *When the Prisoners Ran Walpole*, 18.

65. Hinton, *America on Fire*.

66. Bert Useem and Peter Kimball, *States of Siege: US Prison Riots, 1971– 1986* (New York: Oxford University Press, 1991).

67. Useem and Kimball point to a revolution in rising legal entitlements, popular fears of social disorder, and a general decline in trust of public institutions to explain the diverging outcomes. Unlike the 1950s, unrest in the 1970s resulted in the systematic dismantling of the long-accepted, expert-led rehabilitation paradigm. See Useem and Kimball, *States of Siege*.

CHAPTER 5. ON PRISON DEMOCRACY

"You've got to . . . in order here," epigraph to "March 15 to May 18, 1973": Observer notes, March 28, Shift 3, OPF.

"We want a . . . act like men," epigraph to "March 15 to May 18, 1973": Observer notes, March 17, Shift 2, OPF.

1. This chapter draws from material originally published in Christopher D. Berk, "On Prison Democracy: The Politics of Participation in a Maximum Security Prison," *Critical Inquiry* 44, no. 2 (2018): 275–302.

2. Observer notes, March 15, Shift 1, Observer Program Files (hereafter OPF). I quote extensively from these files in the notes and text so readers can get a sense of the evidence used to support my descriptions and inferences.

3. I follow Kauffman in using the term *prison officer* instead of *guard* or *corrections officer*: "My use of the term 'prison officer' reflects my orientation toward those I studied and their role within prisons. 'Guard' is too suggestive of a static relationship, something one does with inanimate objects. In any case, its connotations are derogatory and belittling. 'Correction officer' conveys a fanciful (and, to my mind, unseemly) notion of the relationship between keeper and kept. 'Prison officer' simply denotes an individual granted official authority within the specific domain of a penal institution." Kelsey Kauffman, *Prison Officers and Their World* (Cambridge, MA: Harvard University Press, 1985), 5.

4. Quoted in Jamie Bissonette, *When the Prisoners Ran Walpole: A True Story in the Movement for Prison Abolition* (Cambridge, MA: South End Press, 2008), 132. After being given the keys, Rodman immediately passed them over to the state police.

5. Kauffman, *Prison Officers and Their World*.

6. Observer notes, March 10, Shift 2, OPF.

7. Jerry Taylor, "Boone Declares Emergency at Walpole as Strike Looms," *Boston Globe*, March 15, 1973, 1.

8. Prison officers were represented by separate locals of the American Federation of State, County, and Municipal Employees (AFSCME, AFL-CIO), and representatives of the locals met monthly in the Penal Committee of Council 41. Philip Heymann et al., "Massachusetts Department of Correction," HKS nos. 165–67 (report, Harvard Kennedy School Cambridge, MA, 1977).

9. John Carver, "Boone Being Undermined," *Boston Globe*, March 17, 1973, 8.

10. Heymann et al., "Massachusetts Department of Correction."

11. Heymann et al., "Massachusetts Department of Correction."

12. The estimate in the official report of the observer program was forty-six hundred hours between March 8 and 25. See "Comments of Observers Present at MCI Walpole, March 8–Mar[ch] 25, 1973," 126. Participation in the program was not constant between March and May; participation was heaviest in the initial weeks of the program. Ten thousand hours is a conservative extrapolation.

13. The only work that makes any reference to the files is Bissonette, *When the Prisoners Ran Walpole*. Howard Zinn describes his personal experience as an observer in Howard Zinn, *Justice in Everyday Life* (Boston: South End Press, 1974). Bissonette's book, coauthored by former NPRA members Robert Dellelo and Ralph Hamm, provided the initial inspiration to examine the observer files.

14. For instance, see Leo Carroll, *Lawful Order: A Case Study of Correctional Crisis and Reform* (New York: Garland, 1999), or for a classic, see John J. DiIulio, *Governing Prisons: A Comparative Study of Correctional Management* (New York: Free Press, 1987).

15. For instance, see Zinn, *Justice in Everyday Life*; J. E. Baker, "Inmate Self-Government and the Right to Participate" in *Correctional Institutions*, ed. Robert Carter, Daniel Glaser, and Leslie Wilkins (Philadelphia: Lippincott, 1977), 320–32; or Bissonette, *When the Prisoners Ran Walpole*.

16. As with democratic theorists generally, most reformers can be arrayed on a spectrum, from liberal to radical, depending on their theoretical priors. David Miller defines the two ends of the spectrum as "R-Democrats" and "L-Democrats." For the former, the value of democracy is best understood instrumentally, in terms of the content of the decisions that will result from following democratic procedures; for the latter, "democracy is valued intrinsically, and the idea of collective self-determination stands at the heart of democratic theory." David Miller, "Democracy's Domain," *Philosophy & Public Affairs* 37, no. 3 (2009): 205. This is not to deny, of course, the existence of various hybrid positions (like the united narrative I describe in this chapter).

17. Observer notes, March 16, Shifts 1–3, OPF.

18. Observer notes, March 16, Shift 1, OPF.

19. Consider the following excerpt: "The place currently is like no other joint in the world (as one young social worker serving as an interim guard put it, 'This is much more important than Woodstock.'). What's happening here is true behavior modification. The prisoner's image of himself is changing radically."

Observer notes, March 18, Shift 3, OPF. And another: "Several claimed that the 'eyes of the country' were on Walpole, and that the inmates were determined to 'pull it off' successfully." Observer notes, March 18, Shift 3, OPF.

20. Observer notes, March 22, Shift 1, OPF. Unfortunately, the prisoner unionization movement during the 1970s is largely ignored in scholarship on prisons. For a recent treatment, see Donald F. Tibbs, *From Black Power to Prison Power: The Making of Jones v. North Carolina* (New York: Palgrave, 2012). DeSalvo was more widely known at the time as "the Boston Strangler."

21. Observer notes, April 4, Shift 2, OPF. This was not just a perception; prison census figures back up this claim: 73.9 percent of prisoners at Walpole did not make it to the twelfth grade. Joseph Higgins, *A Description of the Residents of Massachusetts Correctional Institutions on January 1, 1973* (Massachusetts Department of Corrections, 1973).

22. Observer notes, March 25, Shift 3, OPF.

23. After a month, one increasingly finds references to prisoners being tired of talking to observers. From an interview in the *Boston Globe*: "'The novelty has worn off,' said a long-term inmate who requested anonymity. 'It's getting boring. Wednesday night, all the guys in my block were asleep at nine o'clock. You could hear a pin drop.'" Jerry Taylor, "Walpole: The Prison Where There's Nothing to Do," *Boston Globe*, April 16, 1973, 3.

24. One suggestion that was never realized, for instance, was a prison canteen where profits would be used to fund an area halfway house. Many, many observer reports are dominated by long numbered lists of prisoners' ideas for various reforms.

25. Observer notes, March 30, OPF. One might add, as another observer rightly points out, that "a process of self-selection impacts the informational value of conversations held between an observer and inmates."

26. Observer notes, March 16, Shift 3, OPF; Observer notes, March 18, Shift 3, OPF; and Observer notes, March 16, Shift 3, OPF.

27. In particular, hostility toward the policies of the previous superintendent of Walpole, Raymond Porelle, was a key galvanizing force for the prisoners. In one prisoner's words, "Porelle came in like Wyatt Erp and left the place shaking like a motherfucker." Observer notes, March 18, Shift 2, OPF.

28. Observer notes, March 17, Shift 2, OPF.

29. This exhortation to unity was not an exception; a week later an observer jotted down the following: "NPRA meeting in auditorium—400–500 prisoners—theme was 'we all stick together, black and white, stay cool, cause no incidents, show the world we can control ourselves and we will get concessions. . . . Don't let the "games" the guards play upset anybody—stay cool all the time. We can control ourselves[,] by ourselves.'" Observer notes, March 23, Shift 2, OPF.

30. A few examples: "Several also stated flatly that if the state police where brought in here there would be bloodshed. Perhaps another Attica." Observer notes, March 18, Shift 2, OPF. "More than a few fully expected another Attica." Observer notes, April 5, Shift 2, OPF. "It'll make Attica look like a picnic." Observer notes, May 5, Shift 3, OPF.

31. For example: "Rap with internal board of NPRA—admin propose that the inmates go to work the next day. After much discussion and a vote by the

block captain (13–13) the proposal was taken to the inmate population. They after 45 min voted to go back to work for one week provided negotiations continue in good faith." Observer notes, March 8, Shift 3, OPF. "Inmates in the P.C. [protective custody] corridor told me that senior officer [JL] has been on duty in 10 Block the day shift (7–3) since Tuesday, even though he has been banned from inmate contact by Boone, the NPRA, and the prison administration. They have not been eating any meals since Wednesday." Observer notes, May 5, Shift 2, OPF. "He spoke particularly of his experience on block 9 where people on phase 1 refused to accept any privilege or move to phase 2 unless everyone on phase 1 was granted the privilege." Observer notes, April 10, Shift 3, OPF.

32. For example: "I attended a BANTU meeting (Black American [African] Nation To [Towards] Unity) held in the visiting room. . . . The organization is concerned with helping themselves achieve those [social] services within and without the institution necessary to rehabilitation. . . . The meeting dealt with areas of low education, medicine, medical psychiatric services etc." Observer notes, April 11, Shift 2, OPF.

33. There is a continuous stream of reports of high morale and togetherness among the prisoners between March and May, including the weeks immediately preceding the lockdown. For example: "The prisoners still continue to relate very well to each other and all seem very responsive to both the cadet guards and the observers." Observer notes, May 2, Shift 2, OPF.

34. Consider the following: "One white prisoner remarked during a softball game that too much racial separation exists here and prejudice can be observed even on the ball field. One team was made up of all blacks, the other was all white[,] except one." Observer notes, April 30, Shift 2, OPF.

35. Observer notes, March 27, Shift 2, OPF.

36. See Higgins, "*Description of the Residents of Massachusetts Correctional Institutions.* Also, this is after a decade of internecine Irish mob conflicts and the rising strength of the Italian mob in Boston. The gang network of "Whitey" Bulger was particularly influential. See generally Dick Lehr and Gerard O'Neill, *Black Mass: The Irish Mob, the Boston FBI, and a Devil's Deal* (Oxford: PublicAffairs, 2000).

37. Noted in conversation with Robert Dellelo in February 2013: "Talk about bitter Italian-Irish conflict, Mafia, is now outdated." Observer notes, March 16, Shift 3, OPF.

38. See Ronald Formisano, *Boston against Busing: Race, Class, and Ethnicity in the 1960s and 1970s* (Chapel Hill: University of North Carolina Press, 2004).

39. For more on this point, see Donald Clemmer's masterwork, *The Prison Community* (Boston: Christopher Publishing House, 1940).

40. *Attica: The Official Report of the New York State Special Commission on Attica* (New York: Bantam Books, 1972), 141.

41. While the analysis is not particularly convincing on this point, Heymann et al., "Massachusetts Department of Correction," is illustrative:

This increasing militancy affected traditional inmate social organization and attitudes. First the new political approach contradicted the maxim, "do your own time," to which 'right guys" subscribed and which the correctional staff itself admonished prisoners to follow. Second, the militant politicized prisoner tended to assume the role of "'gorilla," the aggressive inmate who uses violence. Third, [s]uch a prisoner would tend to refuse to cooperate with correctional staff in the traditional network of unofficial contacts and relationships. Taken together, the trends demonstrated a shift in power way from "right guys" and the "thief" subculture toward the "gorillas" and a general erosion of the traditional system of social control (p. 14).

42. Observer notes, March 18, Shift 3, OPF. "One black prisoner informed me that he felt that racial bias was in evidence. He felt that blacks were left out of certain programs." Observer notes, April 7, Shift 3, OPF.

43. John McGrath, a member of the NPRA internal board, is quoted in Bissonette, *When the Prisoners Ran Walpole*:

At first, the discussion revolved around representation of Black prisoners on the board. I advocated for a twenty-seven-member board—nine Black, nine white, and nine Spanish. I kept getting overruled because the white prisoners were afraid that the Blacks and Spanish would unite and overrule them. Eventually, the Spanish guys said they only wanted three representatives because of the small number of Spanish guys in the prison. So the board had twenty-one members—nine Black, nine white, and three Spanish. The guys agreed they would vote from their hearts as men not because of their skin color. And it worked, too. But I really think if I hadn't been so stubborn, it might have fallen apart because the NPRA had to be about equality not about *equal opportunity*. That didn't work on the street and it sure wasn't going to work inside (p. 86).

44. On the initial election of the NPRA board, one observer writes, "I talked to an inmate who said one of the reps asked him about NPRA and was it a viable force; the inmate said yes. Then the rep asked if it was a democratic election. The inmate said yes—as democratic as possible." OPF, Apr 11, Shift 2.

45. Quoted in Bissonette, *When the Prisoners Ran Walpole*, 13.

46. Robert Dellelo, conversation with author, February 2013.

47. Observer notes, March 18, Shift 2, OPF.

48. Quoted in Bissonette, *When the Prisoners Ran Walpole*, 78. See also Peter Remick and James B. Shuman, *In Constant Fear: The Brutal True Story of Life within the Walls of the Notorious Walpole State Prison* (New York: Reader's Digest Press, 1975), 106: "Shortly after the walkout, the NPRA sent out the following verbal message: If an inmate kills an officer or anyone else during the walkout, we've lost and we'll kill that inmate. If an inmate knifes a guard or anyone else during the walkout, that inmate will be knifed. We have too much to lose. We're not playing little kiddy games anymore. We got one hell of a lot to lose."

49. Robert Dellelo, conversation with author, February 2013. On sex offenders: "Feels strongly that you cannot mix all kinds of offenders within one prison. Told me of how some inmates beat up another because he was a sex offender." Observer notes, April 20, Shift 3, OPF.

50. See John Irwin, *The Felon* (Englewood Cliffs, NJ: Prentice-Hall, 1970), 69.

51. Observer notes, May 4, Shift 1, OPF.

52. Randall Conrad and Stephen Ujlaki, dirs., *Three Thousand Years and Life* (Distributor unknown, 1973), 42 min.

53. Observer notes, May 1, Shift 1, OPF.

54. One observer writes: "I noticed that at least 6 persons had Black Eyes, a swollen jaw or cuts on the forehead." Observer notes, April 15, Shift 1, OPF.

55. An observer writes: "A rep. of the NPRA (Jerry Sousa) has told us of a tactical patrol by NPRA to prevent and/or intervene should there be any incidents in halls or blocks." Observer notes, March 27, Shift 1, OPF. See Ralph Hamm quoted in Bissonette, *When the Prisoners Ran Walpole*, 143–45.

56. For example: "Brief trip with [PB] to min avocation area. Several inmates in corridor called out 'cop[,]' moved into Jewelry room. Inmate at grinding wheel was grinding what appeared to be a knife. I did not enter but continued through corridor to Leather, then out. Grinding continued." Observer notes, April 26, Shift 1, OPF.

57. Observer notes, May 3, Shift 2, OPF.

58. This cuts against the claim that a few prisoners, the "wrecking crew," could hold the population in check through fear and brutality. *Carlo v. Gunter*, 392 F. Supp. 871 (D. Mass. 1975).

59. In particular, I have in mind Bernard Harcourt's discussion of discipline within the Occupy Wall Street movement, which in part incorporates fieldwork I conducted as a graduate student. See Bernard E. Harcourt, "Political Disobedience," *Critical Inquiry* 39, no. 2 (2012): 42ff.

60. Observer notes, March 30, Shift 1, OPF.

61. I use the term *narrative* here with purpose. My ambition in the following discussion is less to formalize a narrative sequence for the sake of inference than to make explicit the latent assumptions that underpin that narrative. The plot of the Walpole episode, as narrated in the newspaper coverage and policy discussions reviewed earlier, is a particular application of a wider story about how punishment functions in a liberal-democratic regime. To tell a story about an event is, at least in part, to explain it. A narrative organizes an event in a chronological sequence and channels that sequence into a plot with a beginning, a series of intervening events, and an end, usually to infer cause or interpret meaning. "Plot," according to Ricoeur, is "the intelligible whole that governs a succession of events in any story." Importantly, the narrative mode of comprehension is "configurational," it "puts its elements into a single, concrete complex of relations." See Paul Ricoeur, *Time and Narrative*, trans. Kathleen McLaughlin and David Pellauer (Chicago: University of Chicago Press, 1984), 1.

62. Taylor, "Walpole," 3.

63. Ray Richard, "Guards Call Conditions 'Intolerable,'" *Boston Globe*, March 15, 1973, 1.

64. The Irish and Italian mafias both had influence inside the prison.

65. Heymann et al., "Massachusetts Department of Correction."

66. The Omnibus Prison Reform Act passed in 1972 involved implementing provisions such as a furlough system and the construction of community halfway houses.

67. DiIulio's text is particularly appropriate because the turmoil in Walpole prison in the late 1970s and early 1980s was one of the central motivations for his work.

68. See DiIulio, *Governing Prisons*: "If one is interested in improving the quality of prison life, the best way to think about the prison is not as a mini-society but as a mini-government" (p. 235). Tom Wicker makes a similar note about the organization of prisoners during the Attica rebellion: "When Schwartz and Eve arrived in D-yard about 3 P.M., they found a rough social and political order functioning, although six hours earlier all its inhabitants—alienated, angry men, many of them unschooled, violent, and admitted lawbreakers— had been prisoners of the state of New York, under constant surveillance, and reduced to little more than lockstep circumstances." Tom Wicker, *A Time to Die* (Chicago: Haymarket Books, 2011), 23.

69. DiIulio, *Governing Prisons*, 46.

70. A participatory culture is one with low barriers to expression, support for sharing expression, and informal mentorship for knowledge transfer, and in which members both believe their contributions matter and feel a connection to one another. See Henry Jenkins, *Confronting the Challenges of Participatory Culture: Media Education for the 21st Century* (Cambridge, MA: MIT Press, 2009) and the work of Cathy Cohen and Joseph Kahne.

71. See Jacques Rancière, *Disagreement: Politics and Philosophy* (Minneapolis: University of Minneasota Press, 1999); and DiIulio, *Governing Prisons*, 262.

72. See David Ciepley, "Beyond Public and Private: Toward a Political Theory of the Corporation," *American Political Science Review* 107, no. 1 (2013): 139–58.

73. Loïc Wacquant, *Punishing the Poor: The Neoliberal Government of Social Insecurity* (Durham, NC: Duke University Press, 2009), xviii.

74. See Bernard E. Harcourt, *The Illusion of Free Markets: Punishment and the Myth of Natural Order* (Cambridge, MA: Harvard University Press, 2011). For critics of the relationship between neoliberalism and mass incarceration in the United States, see Michael C. Campbell and Heather Schoenfeld, "The Transformation of America's Penal Order: A Historicized Political Sociology of Punishment," *American Journal of Sociology* 118, no. 5 (2013): 1375–1423; and Nicola Lacey, "Punishment, (Neo)Liberalism and Social Democracy," in *The Sage Handbook of Punishment and Society*, ed. Jonathan Simon and Richard Sparks (Los Angeles: Sage, 2013), 260–80.

75. Again, I take liberal welfarist and liberal law and order claims to be rooted in a set of common assumptions about the shape of civil society's domain (even if there is disagreement about what citizens on the outside owe to prisoners).

76. "Ad Hoc Committee on Prison Reform: Response to WBZ Editorial of March 16, 1973", OPF.

77. Jerry Taylor, "Full Collective Bargaining Rights Sought by Walpole Inmates," *Boston Globe*, April 30, 1973, 4.

78. The full quotation is as follows:

> Through the first months of 1973, citizens stayed inside Walpole for twenty-four hours a day, on three eight-hour shifts, to create a kindlier atmosphere, to try to make sure terrible things did not happen. At the heart of this process of change were the prisoners

themselves, affected in some indescribable way these past years by the revolt at Attica, by the death of George Jackson, by the war in Vietnam, by the general rise of protest in the country. In this process, men, who had not gone in as 'political' prisoners, who had been what we call common criminals, began emerging rehabilitated. But not in the way the government talks of rehabilitation, not obsequiously taking their place in the accepted, legal criminal order of things. Rather as rebels and organizers, as thoughtful, militant men ready to devote their lives to abolishing prisons along with that complexity of conditions that makes prisons seem logical.

Zinn, *Justice in Everyday Life*, 192.

79. For instance: "The goal of the prisoners' union project was two-fold: to exercise self-determination within the prison, and to demonstrate that the prison itself was unnecessary." Bissonette, *When the Prisoners Ran Walpole*, 89.

80. I don't mean to imply the analogy is implausible. Consider Dario Melossi and Massimo Pavarini's classic text *The Prison and the Factory: Origins of the Penitentiary System* (London: Palgrave Macmillan, 2018) or the simple fact that prisoners often work (cleaning, cooking, teaching) within the organizations that confine them.

81. Carole Pateman, *Participation and Democratic Theory* (Cambridge: Cambridge University Press, 1970), 35.

82. Before the strike, for example, the prison administration tried to revive an "inmate grievance council" to serve as a release valve for bubbling prisoner dissatisfaction in the wake of Attica. As discussed in the previous chapter, there is a long and interesting history of the use of inmate councils at Charlestown, then Walpole. To use Pateman's terminology, this form of participation was "pseudo," participation in name only, in which participants had little influence on distributive outcomes within the prison. Similarly, however, the NPRA also used participation as a way to co-opt potentially fractious elements of the prisoner population. While these individuals were full participants (they wielded actual authority), participation by would-be dissenters strategically served a series of ends external to themselves. In effect, they lost influence by becoming participants in the prison regime. In Pateman's work full participation (in contrast to "pseudo" or "partial") comes across as an unadulterated good, but the events at Walpole suggest a more complicated story. Domination and democracy go hand in hand; maximal participation, perhaps counterintuitively, can at times lend aid to domination. Skeptics on the political left argued a version of this point. They claimed, for example, that the prisoners' union was simply mutton dressed as lamb, little more than a traditional "lobbying group for reforms sought by the state itself." Bob Martin, "The Massachusetts Correctional System: Treatment as an Ideology," *Crime and Social Justice* 6 (1976): 52.

83. For a related point about social structure, see Jack A. Goldstone and Bert Useem, "Prison Riots as Microrevolutions: An Extension of State-Centered Theories of Revolution," *American Journal of Sociology* 104, no. 4 (1999): 985–1029.

84. A particularly brutal example of these nested exclusions is prisoner-on-prisoner violence during the notorious 1980 New Mexico prison riot. "Seventeen of the 33 inmates killed were housed in Cell Block 3 and Cell Block 4. Twelve of these inmates were tortured with blow torches, set afire, and mutilated; one was

beheaded with a shovel. The victims included suspected 'snitches,' a child rapist, and 'mentally disturbed' inmates whose screaming had kept other inmates in segregation awake at night." Mark Colvin, "The 1980 New Mexico Prison Riot," *Social Problems* 29, no. 5 (1982): 458.

85. On methodological individualism, see Jon Elster, *Explaining Social Behavior: More Nuts and Bolts for the Social Sciences* (Cambridge: Cambridge University Press, 2007). For criticism, see Andrew Abbott, "Mechanisms and Relations," *Sociologica* 1, no. 2 (2007): 1–22. On ontology, Patchen Markell notes, "For these authors, such efforts go wrong at the level of what we might call social and political 'ontology': they rest on distorted pictures of basic features of the human world, mistaking the irreducible conditions of social and political life for pathologies that might someday be overcome." Patchen Markell, *Bound by Recognition* (Princeton, NJ: Princeton University Press, 2003), 3–4.

86. For a contemporary example, see Martha C. Nussbaum, *Creating Capabilities: The Human Development Approach* (Cambridge, MA: Harvard University Press, 2011).

87. See John F. Padgett and Walter W. Powell, *The Emergence of Organizations and Markets* (Princeton, NJ: Princeton University Press, 2012), 3.

88. Erving Goffman, *Asylums: Essays on the Social Situation of Mental Patients and Other Inmates* (New York: Random House, 1961), 12.

89. First and foremost I have in mind Erving Goffman, but one could also attribute similar approaches to theorists like Michel Foucault and Bruno Latour.

90. "Ad Hoc Committee on Prison Reform: Response to WBZ Editorial of March 16, 1973", OPF.

91. Observer notes, March 25, Shift 1, OPF.

92. William J. Stuntz, *Collapse of American Criminal Justice* (Cambridge, MA: Belknap Harvard University Press, 2011), 311.

93. Michelle Alexander, *The New Jim Crow: Mass Incarceration in the Age of Colorblindness* (New York: New Press, 2010), 258.

94. Angela Yvonne Davis, *The Meaning of Freedom: And Other Difficult Dialogues* (San Francisco: City Lights Books, 2013), 30.

95. Before becoming a preference for peace over war, consensus was a "certain regime of the perceptible: the regime in which the parties are presupposed as already given, their community established and the count of their speech identical to their linguistic performance. What consensus thus presupposes is the disappearance of any gap between a party to a dispute and a part of society. It is the disappearance of the mechanisms of appearance, of the miscount and the dispute opened up by the name 'people' and the vacuum of their freedom." See Rancière, *Disagreement*, 102.

96. "Appearance," Rancière writes, "particularly political appearance, does not conceal reality but in fact splinters it, introduces contentious objects into it, objects whose mode of presentation is not homogeneous with the ordinary mode of existence of the objects thereby identified." Rancière, *Disagreement*, 104.

97. See Daniel Nichanian, "Seizing a Seat at the Table: Participatory Politics and Disqualification" (PhD diss., University of Chicago, 2016); and Glenn David Mackin, *The Politics of Social Welfare in America* (New York: Cambridge University Press, 2013) on this point.

98. In a word, this more radical vision of participatory democracy is neither foundational nor antifoundational, but *non*foundational. This view is in kinship with the discussion of "plantation politics" in Robert Gooding-Williams, *In the Shadow of Du Bois: Afro-Modern Political Thought in America* (Cambridge, MA: Harvard University Press, 2009), 236–37. A plantation politics perspective views resistance as participant based, not expressivist; rather than act on pregiven principles assumed to unite a given group, a participant perspective takes the task of establishing such principles to be a political task in its own right.

99. Consider the following: "I am impressed by the amount of 'inside' control the inmates have. There seemed to be a general concern for image and welfare and consequently the inmates handle themselves in a good manner. Everyone knew what he had to do—whether it be clean up or kitchen help, they did a good job." Observer notes, April 21, Shift 2, OPF. Block counts involve all inmates being locked in their cells for between a half hour and an hour and a half, at least twice a day. Conducting counts quickly and accurately became a source of pride for many block captains. See Observer notes, March 16, Shift 1, OPF.

100. See Observer notes, March 19, 1973, Shift 3, OPF ("fear of REPRISALS is real"). Bissonette, *When the Prisoners Ran Walpole*.

101. Jones v. North Carolina Prisoners' Labor Union, Inc., 433 U.S. 119 (1977).

102. Dan Berger, *Captive Nation: Black Prison Organizing in the Civil Rights Era* (Chapel Hill: University of North Carolina Press, 2014); and Erin Hatton, *Labor and Punishment: Work in and out of Prison* (Oakland: University of California Press, 2021), 73–75.

103. In the 1980s the townspeople decided that they didn't want the city of Walpole to be synonymous with the state's only maximum-security prison, so they held a contest and changed the name from MCI-Walpole to MCI-Cedar Junction, after an abandoned nearby railroad station.

104. David Abel, "Water at State's Largest Prison Raises Concerns," *Boston Globe*, June 17, 2017.

105. Alice Speri, "The Largest Prison Strike in U.S. History Enters Its Second Week," *Intercept*, September 16, 2016.

CHAPTER 6. DEMOCRATIC EROSION

1. See, for instance, Tom Shakespeare's work on the "social model" of disability.

2. Again, the category "ontologically objective" comes from Searle. The account given here, in the context of disability, is broadly consistent with Elizabeth Barnes's "value neutral model." Value neutrality, for instance, does not require denying the bad effects of particular disabilities. "Sure, *some* of the bad effects of disability are caused by social attitudes and social prejudices. But at least for many disabilities, there would be things about them that were difficult or unpleasant even in an ideal society." See Elizabeth Barnes, *The Minority Body: A Theory of Disability* (Oxford: Oxford University Press, 2016), 78ff.

3. The argument for ontological objectivity is simplest in the case of children, more complex in the case of the mad, and probably least persuasive in the case of lawbreakers.

4. The phrase "dumb pipes" is from the network's literature, not mine.

5. See Cathy Cohen, *Democracy Remixed* (Oxford: Oxford University Press, 2011).

6. Consider Padgett and Powell's memorable line: "In the short run actors make relations, but in the long run relations make actors." See generally John F. Padgett and Walter W. Powell, *The Emergence of Organizations and Markets* (Princeton, NJ: Princeton University Press, 2012).

7. Beyond the spark of the intervention by Abrahams and the kindling of the rise of psychotherapy, the war required that the hospital be run in a way that was unreceptive to experimentation and reform.

8. Archon Fung, "Democratic Theory and Political Science: A Pragmatic Method of Constructive Engagement," *American Political Science Review* 101, no. 3 (2007): 444.

9. Fung, "Democratic Theory and Political Science."

10. David Rothman, "Decarcerating Prisoners and Patients," *Civil Liberties Review* 1 (1973): 8–30.

11. See, for example, Ashley Rubin, "A Neo-Institutional Account of Prison Diffusion," *Law & Society Review* 49, no. 2 (2015): 365–400.

12. Albert O. Hirschman, *Exit, Voice, and Loyalty: Responses to Decline in Firms, Organizations and States* (Cambridge, MA: Harvard University Press, 1970). Custodial institutions are the targets of strategic action (perhaps for the "convenience" of actors, perhaps for other ends and ambitions), their supporting conditions dissolve in the face of changing social climates, and new challenges arise for which existing procedures are ill-equipped.

13. Sharon Dolovich, "Cruelty, Prison Conditions, and the Eighth Amendment," *New York University Law Review* 84, no. 4 (2009): 881–979.

14. In short, they embraced publicity. See Jonathan R. Bruno, "Vigilance and Confidence: Jeremy Bentham, Publicity, and the Dialectic of Political Trust and Distrust," *American Political Science Review* 111, no. 2 (2017): 295–307; and Jon Elster, *Securities against Misrule: Juries, Assemblies, Elections* (New York: Cambridge University Press, 2013).

15. Angela Yvonne Davis, *The Meaning of Freedom: And Other Difficult Dialogues* (San Francisco: City Lights Books, 2013).

Bibliography

ARCHIVAL SOURCES

NARA   National Archives and Record Administration, Washington, DC
      E   Entry
      R   Record Group
OPF   Walpole Observer Program Files, Jamie Bissonette Lewey, American
      Friends Service Committee, Cambridge, MA
SEHSC   St. Elizabeths Hospital Special Collections, Washington, DC

A. H. Kiracofe to David Harris, 30 April 1957; Monthly Reports; RG 418,
E 22; NARA.
"Ad Hoc Committee on Prison Reform: Response to WBZ Editorial of March
16, 1973"; OPF.
Anne Bushart to the Superintendent, July 1958; Monthly Reports; RG 418,
E 22; NARA.
Anne Bushart to the Superintendent, October 1958; Monthly Reports; RG 418,
E 22; NARA.
Anne K. Bushart to Winfred Overholser, November 1957; Monthly Report;
RG 418, E 22; NARA.
Anne K. Bushart to Winfred Overholser, May 1958; Monthly Reports; RG 418,
E 22; NARA.
Anne K. Bushart to Winfred Overholser, October 1958; Monthly Reports;
RG 418, E 22; NARA.
"Around the Hall," *Howard Hall Journal* 2, no. 1 (1948): 3; SEHSC.
"Bits of This and That," *Howard Hall Journal* 2, no. 3 (1949): 15; SEHSC.

"The Christmas Season—A Time for Harmony," *John Howard Journal* 17, no. 12 (1965): 5; SEHSC.

"Comments of Observers Present at MCI Walpole, March 8–March 25, 1973," 126; OPF.

"Cooperation," *John Howard Journal* 18, no. 2 (1965): 4; SEHSC.

"Cousin Mot," *John Howard Journal* 18, nos. 5-6 (1966): 41; SEHSC.

"Cover Story," *John Howard Journal* 17, no. 6 (1956): 1; SEHSC.

David Harris to Francis Tartaglino, 6 August 1956; Monthly Reports; RG 418, E 22; NARA.

David Harris to Francis Tartaglino, 6 March 1957; Monthly Reports; RG 418, E 22; NARA.

David Harris to Francis Tartaglino, 5 April 1957; Monthly Reports; RG 418, E 22; NARA.

David Harris to Francis Tartaglino, 3 June 1957; Monthly Reports; RG 418, E 22; NARA.

David Harris to Manson Pettit, 6 April 1959; Monthly Reports; RG 418, E 22; NARA.

David Harris to the Superintendent, 7 July 1959; Annual Reports; RG 418, E 20; NARA.

David Harris to Winfred Overholser, 8 May 1962; Monthly Reports; RG 418, E 22; NARA.

E. D. Griffin to Winfred Overholser, 1 July 1946; Annual Reports; RG 418, E 20; NARA.

"Editorials," *John Howard Journal* 17, no. 11 (1965): 5; SEHSC.

An Elizabethan Anthology. Washington, DC: St. Elizabeths Hospital, 1969, 63; SEHSC.

Evelyn B. Reichenbach to Winfred Overholser, 30 July 1958; Annual Reports; RG 418, E 20; NARA.

Evelyn B. Reichenbach to Winfred Overholser, 4 August 1959; Annual Reports; RG 418, E 20; NARA.

"Exodus Plus Seven," *John Howard Journal* 18, no. 9 (1966): 6; SEHSC.

F. J. Tartaglino to Winfred Overholser, 11 May 1954; Monthly Reports; RG 418, E 22; NARA.

F. J. Tartaglino to Winfred Overholser, 9 July 1955; Annual Reports; RG 418, E 20; NARA.

Francis J. Tartaglino to Winfred Overholser, 15 July 1957; Annual Reports; RG 418, E 20; NARA.

"Group Therapy," *Howard Hall Journal* 2, no. 3 (1949): 4; SEHSC.

Hobbs, William. "Role of Group Psychotherapy in an Admission Service," *Bulletin: A Journal of Group Work at St. Elizabeths Hospital* 5, nos. 1–2 (1961): 4; SEHSC.

Jay Hoffman to Winfred Overholser, 9 November 1954; Monthly Reports; RG 418, E 22; NARA.

Jay Hoffman to Winfred Overholser, 27 November 1956; Monthly Reports; RG 418, E 22; NARA.

Jay Hoffman to Winfred Overholser, 24 April 1957; Monthly Reports; RG 418, E 22; NARA.

Jay L. Hoffman to Winfred Overholser, 23 August 1955; Monthly Reports, 1906–1967; Monthly Reports; RG 418, E 22; NARA.

Jerome Kavka to Addison M. Duval, March 1946; Monthly Reports; RG 418, E 22; NARA.

Joseph Abrahams to B. A. Cruvant [margin note], 30 December 1946; Monthly Reports; RG 418, E 22; NARA.

Joseph Abrahams to Winfred Overholser, March 1948; Monthly Reports; RG 418, E 22; NARA.

Joseph Abrahams to Winfred Overholser, 6 July 1949; Monthly Reports; RG 418, E 22; NARA.

Joseph Abrahams to Winfred Overholser, 22 July 1954; Annual Reports; RG 418, E 20, NARA.

"Lost Sheep," *Howard Hall Journal* 1, no. 3 (1948): 2–3; SEHSC.

Manson B. Pettit to Winfred Overholser, 14 July 1959; Annual Reports; RG 418, E 20; NARA.

"Monthly Journal Is Outlet for the Violently Insane"; Monthly Reports; RG 418, E 22; NARA.

"Needs of the Hospital" in Annual Report of Saint Elizabeths Hospital for the Fiscal Year 1947; Annual Reports; RG 418, E 20; NARA.

Observer notes, 8 March 1973; Shift 3; OPF.

Observer notes, 10 March 1973; Shift 2; OPF.

Observer notes, 15 March 1973; Shift 1; OPF.

Observer notes, 16 March 1973; Shift 1; OPF.

Observer notes, 16 March 1973; Shift 2; OPF.

Observer notes, 16 March 1973; Shift 3; OPF.

Observer notes, 17 March 1973; Shift 2; OPF.

Observer notes, 18 March 1973; Shift 2; OPF.

Observer notes, 18 March 1973; Shift 3; OPF.

Observer notes, 19 March 1973; Shift 3; OPF.

Observer notes, 22 March 1973; Shift 1; OPF.

Observer notes, 23 March 1973; Shift 2; OPF.

Observer notes, 25 March 1973; Shift 1; OPF.

Observer notes, 25 March 1973; Shift 3; OPF.

Observer notes, 27 March 1973; Shift 1; OPF.

Observer notes, 27 March 1973; Shift 2; OPF.

Observer notes, 28 March 1973; Shift 3; OPF.

Observer notes, 30 March 1973; Shift 1; OPF.

Observer notes, 4 April 1973; Shift 2; OPF.

Observer notes, 5 April 1973; Shift 2; OPF.

Observer notes, 7 April 1973; Shift 3; OPF.

Observer notes, 10 April 1973; Shift 3; OPF.

Observer notes, 11 April 1973; Shift 2; OPF.

Observer notes, 15 April 1973; Shift 1; OPF.

Observer notes, 20 April 1973; Shift 3; OPF.

Observer notes, 21 April 1973; Shift 2; OPF.

Observer notes, 26 April 1973; Shift 1; OPF.

Observer notes, 30 April 1973; Shift 2; OPF.

Observer notes, 1 May 1973; Shift 1; OPF.
Observer notes, 2 May 1973; Shift 2; OPF.
Observer notes, 3 May 1973; Shift 2; OPF.
Observer notes, 4 May 1973; Shift 1; OPF.
Observer notes, 5 May 1973; Shift 2; OPF.
Observer notes, 5 May 1973; Shift 3; OPF.
"PAC Report," *John Howard Journal* 17, no. 2 (1964); SEHSC.
Peterson, Arnold. "Report on the Survey of Group Activities." *Bulletin: A Journal of Group Work at St. Elizabeths Hospital* 1, no. 1 (1957); SEHSC.
"Psychiatric Services," in Annual Report of St. Elizabeths Hospital for the Fiscal Year 1947; Annual Reports; RG 418, E 20; NARA.
Report submitted to Addison M. Duval, April 1946; Monthly Reports; RG 418; E 22; NARA.
Roscoe W. Hall to Winfred Overholser, 30 August 1946; Annual Reports; RG 48, E 20; NARA.
Steven Klinger to the Superintendent, 6 July 1959; Annual Reports; RG 418, E 20; NARA.
"Speaking Out," *John Howard Journal* 20, no. 10 (1968): 11; SEHSC.
"St. Elizabeths Hospital," in *Annual Report of the U.S. Department of Health, Education, and Welfare* (1957): 3; SEHSC.
To David J. Owens, 17 May 1962; Monthly Reports; RG 418, E 22; NARA.
To the Superintendent, 1 July 1957; Monthly Reports; RG 418, E 22; NARA.
To the Superintendent, 5 July 1957; Annual Reports; RG 418, E 20; NARA.
To the Superintendent, 11 July 1958; Monthly Reports; RG 418, E 22; NARA.
To Winfred Overholser, 30 July 1958; Annual Reports; RG 418, E 20; NARA.
To Winfred Overholser, 30 July 1958; Monthly Reports; RG 418, E 22; NARA.
To Winfred Overholser, 9 July 1960; Annual Reports; RG 418, E 20; NARA.
"Together or Apart—The Choice is Your[s]," *John Howard Journal* 17, no. 12 (1965): 20; SEHSC.
William Cushard to Superintendent, 1 July 1954; Annual Reports; RG 418, E 20; NARA.
William Cushard to the Superintendent, 1 July 1955; Annual Reports; RG 418, E 20; NARA.
William Cushard to the Superintendent, 2 July 1956; Annual Reports; RG 418, E 20; NARA.
William Cushard to the Superintendent, 6 December 1956; Monthly Reports; RG 418, E 22; NARA.
William Cushard to Winfred Overholser, 1 July 1954; Annual Reports; RG 418, E 20; NARA.
Winfred Overholser, foreword to the Annual Report of 1947; Annual Reports; RG 418, E 20; NARA.

PUBLISHED SOURCES

Abbott, Andrew. "Mechanisms and Relations." *Sociologica* 1, no. 2 (2007): 1–22.

———. *The System of Professions: An Essay on the Division of Expert Labor.* Chicago: University of Chicago Press, 1988.

Abel, David. "Water at State's Largest Prison Raises Concerns." *Boston Globe,* June 17, 2017.

Abizadeh, Arash. "Does Collective Identity Presuppose an Other? On the Alleged Incoherence of Global Solidarity." *American Political Science Review* 99, no. 1 (2005): 45–60.

———. "On the Demos and Its Kin: Nationalism, Democracy, and the Boundary Problem." *American Political Science Review* 106, no. 4 (2012): 867–82.

Abrahams, Joseph. *A Passionate Psychoanalyst: Poems and Dreams.* Bloomington, IN: Xlibris Corporation, 2007.

———. "Preliminary Report of an Experience in the Group Psychotherapy of Schizophrenics." *American Journal of Psychiatry* 104, no. 10 (1948): 613–17.

———. *This Way Out: A Narrative of Therapy with Psychotic and Sexual Offenders.* Vol. 1. Lanham, MD: University Press of America, 2010.

———. *This Way Out: A Narrative of Therapy with Psychotic and Sexual Offenders.* Vol. 2. Lanham, MD: University Press of America, 2010.

Alexander, Michelle. *The New Jim Crow: Mass Incarceration in the Age of Colorblindness.* New York: New Press, 2010.

Altshuler, Alan. *Community Control: The Black Demand for Participation.* New York: Pegasus Press, 1970.

Anderson, Carol. *White Rage: The Unspoken Truth of Our Racial Divide.* New York: Bloomsbury Publishing USA, 2016.

Anderson, Elizabeth. *Private Government.* Princeton, NJ: Princeton University Press, 2017.

Archard, David. *Children: Rights and Childhood.* New York: Routledge, 2004.

Attica: The Official Report of the New York State Special Commission on Attica. New York: Bantam Books, 1972.

Austin, John L. "A Plea for Excuses: The Presidential Address." *Proceedings of the Aristotelian Society* 57 (1956): 1–30.

Bachrach, Peter, and Morton Baratz. "Two Faces of Power." *American Political Science Review* 56, no. 4 (1962): 947–52.

Baker, J. E. "Inmate Self-Government and the Right to Participate." In *Correctional Institutions,* edited by Robert Carter, Daniel Glaser, and Leslie Wilkins, 320–32. Philadelphia, PA: Lippincott, 1977.

———. *Prisoner Participation in Prison Power.* Metuchen, NJ: Scarecrow Press, 1985.

———. *The Right to Participate: Inmate Involvement in Prison Administration.* Metuchen, NJ: Scarecrow Press, 1974.

Barber, Benjamin R. *Strong Democracy: Participatory Politics for a New Age.* Berkeley: University of California Press, 1984.

Barnes, Elizabeth. *The Minority Body: A Theory of Disability.* Oxford: Oxford University Press, 2016.

Benhabib, Seyla. *The Rights of Others: Aliens, Residents, and Citizens.* Cambridge: Cambridge University Press, 2004.

Ben-Moshe, Liat, Chris Chapman, and Allison C. Carey, eds. *Disability Incarcerated: Imprisonment and Disability in the United States and Canada.* New York: Palgrave Macmillan, 2014.

Berger, Dan. *Captive Nation: Black Prison Organizing in the Civil Rights Era.* Chapel Hill, NC: University of North Carolina Press, 2014.

Berger, Dan, and Toussaint Losier. *Rethinking the American Prison Movement.* New York: Routledge, 2017.

Berk, Christopher D. "Must Penal Law Be Insulated from Public Influence?" *Law and Philosophy* 40, no. 1 (2021): 67–87.

———. "On Prison Democracy: The Politics of Participation in a Maximum Security Prison." *Critical Inquiry* 44, no. 2 (2018): 275–302.

Bird, Colin. "Political Theory and Ordinary Language: A Road Not Taken." *Polity* 43, no. 1 (2011): 106–27.

Bissonette, Jamie. *When the Prisoners Ran Walpole: A True Story in the Movement for Prison Abolition.* Cambridge, MA: South End Press, 2008.

Blake, Michael. "Distributive Justice, State Coercion, and Autonomy." *Philosophy & Public Affairs* 30, no. 3 (2001): 257–96.

Boston Globe. "Grossman Listens for Hour in Prison to Convicts' Demands." July 23, 1952, 14.

Braithwaite, John. *Restorative Justice & Responsive Regulation.* Studies in Crime and Public Policy. Oxford: Oxford University Press, 2002.

Braslow, Joel Tupper. "The Manufacture of Recovery." *Annual Review of Clinical Psychology* 9 (2013): 781–809.

Brubaker, Rogers. *Trans: Gender and Race in an Age of Unsettled Identities.* Princeton, NJ: Princeton University Press, 2016.

Bruno, Jonathan R. "Vigilance and Confidence: Jeremy Bentham, Publicity, and the Dialectic of Political Trust and Distrust." *American Political Science Review* 111, no. 2 (2017): 295–307.

Burgess, Ernest W., Joseph D. Lohman, and Clifford R. Shaw. "The Chicago Area Project." In *Coping with Crime,* edited by Marjorie Bell, 8–28. New York: Yearbook of the National Probation and Parole Association, 1937.

Calavita, Kitty, and Valerie Jenness. *Appealing to Justice: Prisoner Grievances, Rights, and Carceral Logic.* Oakland: University of California Press, 2014.

Campbell, Michael C., and Heather Schoenfeld. "The Transformation of America's Penal Order: A Historicized Political Sociology of Punishment." *American Journal of Sociology* 118, no. 5 (2013): 1375–1423.

Carroll, Leo. *Lawful Order: A Case Study of Correctional Crisis and Reform.* New York: Garland, 1999.

Carver, John. "Boone Being Undermined." *Boston Globe,* March 17, 1973, 8.

Cazenave, Noel A. *Impossible Democracy: The Unlikely Success of the War on Poverty Community Action Programs.* Albany: State University of New York Press, 2007.

Chamberlin, Judi. *On Our Own: Patient-Controlled Alternatives to the Mental Health System.* New York: McGraw-Hill, 1978.

Cholbi, Michael J. "A Felon's Right to Vote." *Law and Philosophy* 21, nos. 4–5 (2002): 543–65.

Christiano, Thomas. *The Constitution of Equality*. Oxford: Oxford University Press, 2008.

Ciepley, David. "Beyond Public and Private: Toward a Political Theory of the Corporation." *American Political Science Review* 107, no. 1 (2013): 139–58.

Clemmer, Donald. *The Prison Community*. Boston: Christopher Publishing House, 1940.

Cohen, Cathy. *Democracy Remixed*. Oxford: Oxford University Press, 2011.

Cohen, Cathy, and Joseph Kahne. *Participatory Politics: New Media and Youth Political Action*. Chicago: MacArthur Research Network on Youth and Participatory Politics, 2012.

Cohen, Elizabeth F. *Semi-Citizenship in Democratic Politics*. Cambridge: Cambridge University Press, 2009.

Colvin, Mark. "The 1980 New Mexico Prison Riot." *Social Problems* 29, no. 5 (1982): 449–63.

Comfort, Megan. *Doing Time Together: Love and Family in the Shadow of the Prison*. Chicago: University of Chicago Press, 2008.

Conrad, Randall, and Stephen Ujlaki, dirs. *Three Thousand Years and Life*. Distributor unknown, 1973. 42 minutes.

Cruikshank, Barbara. *The Will to Empower: Democratic Citizens and Other Subjects*. Ithaca, NY: Cornell University Press, 1999.

Cruvant, Bernard A. "The Function of the Administrative Group in a Mental Hospital Group Therapy Program." *American Journal of Psychiatry* 110, no. 5 (1953): 342–46.

———. "Maximum Security and the Therapeutic Milieu." *Psychiatric Services* 3, no. 6 (1952): 6–7.

Cutler, Samuel. "Prisoners at Norfolk Reassured by Doyle." *Boston Globe*, March 2, 1946, 1.

Dahl, Robert. *Democracy and Its Critics*. New Haven, CT: Yale University Press, 1989.

———. *A Preface to Economic Democracy*. Berkeley: University of California Press, 1985.

D'Antonio, Michael. *The State Boys Rebellion*. New York: Simon & Schuster, 2004.

Davis, Angela Y. "Incarcerated Women: Transformative Strategies." *Black Renaissance* 1, no. 1 (1996): 21.

———. *Are Prisons Obsolete?* New York: Seven Stories Press, 2003.

———. *The Meaning of Freedom: And Other Difficult Dialogues*. San Francisco: City Lights Books, 2013.

DiIulio, John J. *Governing Prisons: A Comparative Study of Correctional Management*. New York: Free Press, 1987.

Dillingham, David D., and Linda R. Singer. *Complaint Procedures in Prisons and Jails: An Examination of Recent Experience*. Washington, DC: US Department of Justice, National Institute of Corrections, 1980.

Dilts, Andrew. *Punishment and Inclusion*. New York: Fordham University Press, 2014.

———. "To Kill a Thief: Punishment, Proportionality, and Criminal Subjectivity in Locke's Second Treatise." *Political Theory* 40, no. 1 (2012): 58–83.

Dolovich, Sharon. "Cruelty, Prison Conditions, and the Eighth Amendment." *New York University Law Review* 84, no. 4 (2009): 881–979.

Doris, John M. *Lack of Character: Personality and Moral Behavior.* Cambridge: Cambridge University Press, 2002.

Dryzek, John S. "Policy Sciences of Democracy." *Polity* 22, no. 1 (1989): 97–118.

Duff, Antony. *Punishment, Communication, and Community.* New York: Oxford University Press, 2001.

Dula, Annette. "African American Suspicion of the Healthcare System Is Justified: What Do We Do about It?" *Cambridge Quarterly of Healthcare Ethics* 3, no. 3 (1994): 347–57.

Dumm, Thomas L. *Democracy and Punishment: Disciplinary Origins of the United States.* Madison: University of Wisconsin Press, 1987.

Dzur, Albert. *Democracy Inside: Participatory Innovation in Unlikely Places.* New York: Oxford University Press, 2019.

———. "Participatory Democracy and Criminal Justice." *Criminal Law and Philosophy* 6, no. 2 (2012): 115–29.

Elster, Jon. *Explaining Social Behavior: More Nuts and Bolts for the Social Sciences.* Cambridge: Cambridge University Press, 2007.

———. *Securities against Misrule: Juries, Assemblies, Elections.* New York: Cambridge University Press, 2013.

Formisano, Ronald. *Boston against Busing: Race, Class, and Ethnicity in the 1960s and 1970s.* Chapel Hill: University of North Carolina Press, 2004.

Foucault, Michel. *Discipline and Punish: The Birth of the Prison.* New York: Vintage Books, 1995.

Fraser, Nancy. "Abnormal Justice." *Critical Inquiry* 34, no. 3 (2008): 393–422.

Freeman, Jo. "The Tyranny of Structurelessness." *Berkeley Journal of Sociology* 17 (1972): 151–64.

Fung, Archon. "Democratic Theory and Political Science: A Pragmatic Method of Constructive Engagement." *American Political Science Review* 101, no. 3 (2007): 443–58.

Gambino, Matthew. "Erving Goffman's Asylums and Institutional Culture in the Mid-Twentieth-Century United States." *Harvard Review of Psychiatry* 21, no. 1 (2013): 52–57.

———. "Mental Health and Ideals of Citizenship: Patient Care at St. Elizabeths Hospital in Washington, DC, 1903–1962." PhD thesis, University of Illinois at Urbana-Champaign, 2010.

Garfinkel, Harold. *Studies in Ethnomethodology.* Cambridge, UK: Polity Press, 1984.

Goffman, Erving. *Asylums: Essays on the Social Situation of Mental Patients and Other Inmates.* New York: Random House, 1961.

Goldstone, Jack A., and Bert Useem. "Prison Riots as Microrevolutions: An Extension of State-Centered Theories of Revolution." *American Journal of Sociology* 104, no. 4 (1999): 985–1029.

Goodin, Robert E. "Enfranchising All Affected Interests, and Its Alternatives." *Philosophy & Public Affairs* 35, no. 1 (2007): 40–68.

————. "Inclusion and Exclusion." *European Journal of Sociology* 37, no. 2 (1996): 343–71.

————. "What Is So Special about Our Fellow Countrymen?" *Ethics* 98, no. 4 (1988): 663–86.

Gooding-Williams, Robert. *In the Shadow of Du Bois: Afro-Modern Political Thought in America.* Cambridge, MA: Harvard University Press, 2009.

Gortler, Shai. "Participatory Panopticon: Thomas Mott Osborne's Prison Democracy." *Constellations: An International Journal of Critical and Democratic Theory* 29, no. 3(2022): 343–58.

Gottschalk, Marie. *Caught: The Prison State and the Lockdown of American Politics.* Princeton, NJ: Princeton University Press, 2015.

————. *The Prison and the Gallows: The Politics of Mass Incarceration in America.* New York: Cambridge University Press, 2006.

Graeber, David. *The Democracy Project: A History, a Crisis, a Movement.* New York: Random House, 2013.

Grob, Gerald N. *The Mad among Us: A History of the Care of America's Mentally Ill.* New York: Free Press, 1994.

Guerra, Eliana. "Citizenship Knows No Age: Children's Participation in the Governance and Municipal Budget of Barra Mansa, Brazil." *Environment and Urbanization* 14, no. 2 (2002): 71–84.

Gusfield, Joseph R. *The Culture of Public Problems: Drinking-Driving and the Symbolic Order.* Chicago: University of Chicago Press, 1981.

Hall, Stuart. "Whose Heritage? Un-Settling 'the Heritage', Re-Imagining the Post-Nation." In *The Politics of Heritage,* edited by Jo Littler and Roshi Naidoo, 21–31. London: Routledge, 2005.

Halpern, Robert. *Rebuilding the Inner City: A History of Neighborhood Initiatives to Address Poverty in the United States.* New York: Columbia University Press, 1995.

Harcourt, Bernard E. "Carceral Imaginations." *Carceral Notebooks* 1 (2005): 3–19.

————. *The Illusion of Free Markets: Punishment and the Myth of Natural Order.* Cambridge, MA: Harvard University Press, 2011.

————. *Language of the Gun: Youth, Crime, and Public Policy.* Chicago: University of Chicago Press, 2006.

————. "Political Disobedience." *Critical Inquiry* 39, no. 2 (2012): 42ff.

Hardy, Jeffrey. *The Gulag after Stalin.* Ithaca, NY: Cornell University Press, 2016.

Hatton, Erin. *Labor and Punishment: Work in and out of Prison.* Oakland: University of California Press, 2021.

Heymann, Philip, Alan Konefsky, Richard Peers, and Donald Simon. "Massachusetts Department of Correction." HKS nos. 165–67.. Report, Harvard Kennedy School, Cambridge, MA, 1977. https://case.hks.harvard.edu /massachusetts-department-of-correction-part-i/.

Higgins, Joseph. *A Description of the Residents of Massachusetts Correctional Institutions on January 1, 1973.* Massachusetts Department of Corrections, 1973.

Hinton, Elizabeth. *America on Fire: The Untold History of Police Violence and Black Rebellion Since the 1960s.* New York: Liveright, 2021.

————. *From the War on Poverty to the War on Crime*. Cambridge, MA: Harvard University Press, 2016.

————. "Turn Prisons into Colleges." *New York Times*, March 6, 2018.

Hirschman, Albert O. *Exit, Voice, and Loyalty: Responses to Decline in Firms, Organizations and States*. Cambridge, MA: Harvard University Press, 1970.

Honig, Bonnie. *Emergency Politics: Paradox, Law, Democracy*. Princeton, NJ: Princeton University Press, 2009.

Irwin, John. *The Felon*. Englewood Cliffs, NJ: Prentice-Hall, 1970.

————. *Prisons in Turmoil*. Boston: Little, Brown, 1980.

Jacobs, James. *Stateville: The Penitentiary in Mass Society*. Chicago: University of Chicago Press, 1977.

Jenkins, Henry. *Confronting the Challenges of Participatory Culture: Media Education for the 21st Century*. Cambridge, MA: MIT Press, 2009.

Jones, Maxwell. *The Therapeutic Community: A New Treatment Method in Psychiatry*. New York: Basic Books, 1953.

Kauffman, Kelsey. *Prison Officers and Their World*. Cambridge, MA: Harvard University Press, 1985.

Kleinfeld, Laura I., Joshua Appleman, and Thomas F. Geraghty. "White Paper of Democratic Criminal Justice." *Northwestern University Law Review* 111 (2016): 1693–1705.

Lacey, Nicola. *The Prisoners' Dilemma*. Cambridge: Cambridge University Press, 2008.

————. "Punishment, (Neo)Liberalism and Social Democracy." In *The Sage Handbook of Punishment and Society*, edited by Jonathan Simon and Richard Sparks, 260–80. Los Angeles: Sage, 2013.

Lehr, Dick, and Gerard O'Neill. *Black Mass: The Irish Mob, the Boston FBI, and a Devil's Deal*. Oxford, UK: PublicAffairs, 2000.

Lerman, Amy, and Vesla Weaver. *Arresting Citizenship: The Democratic Consequences of American Crime Control*. Chicago: University of Chicago Press, 2014.

Lewis, Bradley. "A Mad Fight: Psychiatry and Disability Activism." In *The Disability Studies Reader*, edited by Lennard Davis, 339–54. New York: Routledge, 2006.

Lin, Ann Chih. *Reform in the Making: The Implementation of Social Policy in Prison*. Princeton, NJ: Princeton University Press, 2000.

López-Guerra, Claudio. *Democracy and Disenfranchisement: The Morality of Electoral Exclusions*. New York: Oxford University Press, 2014.

Mackin, Glenn. "Inventing Democratic Subjectivity in the 1960s Community Action Programs." *New Political Science* 42, no. 1 (2020): 52–69.

Mackin, Glenn David. *The Politics of Social Welfare in America*. New York: Cambridge University Press, 2013.

Mansbridge, Jane J. *Beyond Adversary Democracy*. New York: Basic Books, 1980.

Markell, Patchen. *Bound by Recognition*. Princeton, NJ: Princeton University Press, 2003.

Martin, Bob. "The Massachusetts Correctional System: Treatment as an Ideology." *Crime and Social Justice* 6 (1976): 49–57.

Melossi, Dario, and Massimo Pavarini. *The Prison and the Factory: Origins of the Penitentiary System*. London: Palgrave Macmillan, 2018.

Metzl, Jonathan. *The Protest Psychosis: How Schizophrenia Became a Black Disease*. Boston: Beacon Press, 2009.

Metzl, Jonathan M., and Kenneth T. MacLeish. "Mental Illness, Mass Shootings, and the Politics of American Firearms." *American Journal of Public Health* 105, no. 2 (2015): 240.

Miller, David. "Democracy's Domain." *Philosophy & Public Affairs* 37, no. 3 (2009): 201–28.

———. "Why Immigration Controls Are Not Coercive: A Reply to Arash Abizadeh." *Political Theory* 38, no. 1 (2010): 111–20.

Moynihan, Daniel P. *Maximum Feasible Misunderstanding*. New York: Free Press, 1969.

Murakawa, Naomi. *The First Civil Right: How Liberals Built Prison America*. Oxford: Oxford University Press, 2014.

Murakawa, Naomi, and Katherine Beckett. "The Penology of Racial Innocence: The Erasure of Racism in the Study and Practice of Punishment." *Law & Society Review* 44, nos. 3–4 (2010): 695–730.

Murton, Tom, and Joe Hyams. *Accomplices to the Crime*. New York: Grove Press, 1969.

Nichanian, Daniel. "Seizing a Seat at the Table: Participatory Politics and Disqualification." PhD diss., University of Chicago, 2016.

Nussbaum, Martha. *Frontiers of Justice: Disability, Nationality, Species Membership*. Cambridge, MA: Harvard University Press, 2006.

Nussbaum, Martha C. *Creating Capabilities: The Human Development Approach*. Cambridge, MA: Harvard University Press, 2011.

Olson, Joel. "Whiteness and the Participation-Inclusion Dilemma." *Political Theory* 30, no. 3 (2002): 384–409.

Padgett, John F., and Walter W. Powell. *The Emergence of Organizations and Markets*. Princeton, NJ: Princeton University Press, 2012.

Pateman, Carole. *Participation and Democratic Theory*. Cambridge: Cambridge University Press, 1970.

Pitts, Jennifer. *Boundaries of the International: Law and Empire*. Cambridge, MA: Harvard University Press, 2018).

Rancière, Jacques. *Disagreement: Politics and Philosophy*. Minneapolis: University of Minnesota Press, 1999.

Reiss, Benjamin. *Theaters of Madness: Insane Asylums and Nineteenth-Century American Culture*. Chicago: University of Chicago Press, 2008.

Rembis, Michael. "The New Asylums: Madness and Mass Incarceration in the Neoliberal Era." In *Disability Incarcerated: Imprisonment and Disability in the United States and Canada*, edited by Liat Ben-Moshe, Chris Chapman, and Allison C. Carey, 139–59. New York: Palgrave Macmillan, 2014.

Remick, Peter, and James B. Shuman. *In Constant Fear: The Brutal True Story of Life within the Walls of the Notorious Walpole State Prison*. New York: Reader's Digest Press, 1975.

Richard, Ray. "Guards Call Conditions 'Intolerable.'" *Boston Globe*, March 15, 1973, 1.

Ricoeur, Paul. *Time and Narrative*. Vol. 1. Translated by Kathleen McLaughlin and David Pellauer. Chicago: University of Chicago Press, 1984.

Roth, Alisa. *Insane: America's Criminal Treatment of Mental Illness*. New York: Basic Books, 2018.

Rothman, David. *Conscience and Convenience: The Asylum and Its Alternatives in Progressive America*. New York: Walter de Gruyter, 2002.

———. "Decarcerating Prisoners and Patients." *Civil Liberties Review* 1 (1973): 8–30.

———. *The Discovery of the Asylum: Social Order and Disorder in the New Republic*. New York: Aldine Transaction, 2002.

Rubenstein, Robert, and Harold Lasswell. *The Sharing of Power in a Psychiatric Hospital*. New Haven, CT: Yale University Press, 1966.

Rubin, Ashley. "A Neo-Institutional Account of Prison Diffusion." *Law & Society Review* 49, no. 2 (2015): 365–400.

Searle, John. *Making the Social World: The Structure of Human Civilization*. New York: Oxford University Press, 2010.

Sewell, William H. "A Theory of Structure: Duality, Agency, and Transformation." *American Journal of Sociology* 98, no. 1 (1992): 1–29.

Shachar, Ayelet, and Ran Hirschl. "On Citizenship, States, and Markets." *Journal of Political Philosophy* 22, no. 2 (2014): 231–57.

Shakespeare, Tom. "The Social Model of Disability." In *The Disability Studies Reader*, edited by Lennard Davis, 195–203. New York: Routledge, 2006.

Shapiro, Ian. *Democratic Justice*. New Haven, CT: Yale University Press, 2001.

Shapiro, Ian, and Casiano Hacker-Cordón. "Outer Edges and Inner Edges." In *Democracy's Edges*, edited by Ian Shapiro, 1–16. Cambridge: Cambridge University Press, 1999.

Shklar, Judith N. *American Citizenship: The Quest for Inclusion*. Cambridge, MA: Harvard University Press, 1991.

Silva, Jennifer M. "Constructing Adulthood in an Age of Uncertainty." *American Sociological Review* 77, no. 4 (2012): 505–22.

Simon, Jonathan. *Mass Incarceration on Trial: A Remarkable Court Decision and the Future of Prisons in America*. New York: New Press, 2014.

Simplican, Stacy Clifford. *The Capacity Contract*. Minneapolis: University of Minnesota Press, 2015.

Skarbek, David. "Governance and Prison Gangs." *American Political Science Review* 105, no. 4 (2011): 702–16.

———. *The Puzzle of Prison Order: Why Life Behind Bars Varies around the World*. New York: Oxford University Press, 2020.

Slobogin, Christopher. *Just Algorithms: Using Science to Reduce Mass Incarceration and Inform a Jurisprudence of Risk*. New York: Cambridge University Press, 2021.

Song, Sarah. "The Boundary Problem in Democratic Theory: Why the Demos Should Be Bounded by the State." *International Theory* 4, no. 1 (2012): 39–68.

Soss, Joe. *Unwanted Claims: The Politics of Participation in the Us Welfare System*. Ann Arbor: University of Michigan Press, 2002.

Spade, Dean. *Mutual Aid: Building Solidarity during This Crisis (and the Next)*. London: Verso Books, 2020.

Speri, Alice. "The Largest Prison Strike in Us History Enters Its Second Week." *Intercept*, September 16, 2016.

Spingarn, Natalie. "St. Elizabeths: Pace-Setter for Mental Hospitals." *Harper's Magazine*, January 1956, 58–63.

Stastny, Charles, and Gabrielle Tyrnauer. *Who Rules the Joint? The Changing Political Culture of Maximum-Security Prisons in America*. Lexington, KY: Lexington Books, 1982.

Staszak, Sarah. *No Day in Court: Access to Justice and the Politics of Judicial Retrenchment*. New York: Oxford University Press, 2014.

Stuntz, William J. *Collapse of American Criminal Justice*. Cambridge, MA: Belknap Harvard University Press, 2011.

Summers, Martin. *Madness in the City of Magnificent Intentions: A History of Race and Mental Illness in the Nation's Capital*. New York: Oxford University Press, 2019.

Sykes, Gresham M. *The Society of Captives: A Study of a Maximum Security Prison*. Princeton, NJ: Princeton University Press, 1958.

Taylor, Charles. *Dilemmas and Connections: Selected Essays*. Cambridge, MA: Harvard University Press, 2011.

Taylor, Jerry. "Boone Declares Emergency at Walpole as Strike Looms." *Boston Globe*, March 15, 1973, 1.

———. "Full Collective Bargaining Rights Sought by Walpole Inmates." *Boston Globe*, April 30, 1973, 4.

———. "Walpole: The Prison Where There's Nothing to Do." *Boston Globe*, April 16, 1973, 3.

Thompson, Heather Ann. *Blood in the Water: The Attica Prison Uprising of 1971 and Its Legacy*. New York: Vintage, 2017.

Tibbs, Donald. *From Black Power to Prison Power: The Making of Jones v. North Carolina*. New York: Palgrave, 2012.

Time Magazine. "The Siege of Cherry Hill." January 31, 1955, 17.

Tribe, Laurence H. "Policy Science: Analysis or Ideology?" *Philosophy & Public Affairs* 2, no. 1 (1972): 66–110.

Tytell, John. *The Solitary Volcano*. New York: Anchor Doubleday, 1987.

Useem, Bert, and Peter Kimball. *States of Siege: US Prison Riots, 1971–1986*. New York: Oxford University Press, 1991.

Wacquant, Loïc. *Punishing the Poor: The Neoliberal Government of Social Insecurity*. Durham, NC: Duke University Press, 2009.

Way, Bruce B., Donald A. Sawyer, Stephanie N. Lilly, Catherine Moffitt, and Barbara J. Stapholz. "Characteristics of Inmates Who Received a Diagnosis of Serious Mental Illness upon Entry to New York State Prison." *Psychiatric Services* 59, no. 11 (2008): 1335–37.

Weaver, Vesla, and Amy Lerman. "A Trade-Off between Safety and Democracy? An Empirical Investigation of Prison Violence and Inmate Self-Governance." In *Democratic Theory and Mass Incarceration*, edited by Albert W. Dzur, Ian Loader, and Richard Sparks, 238–65. Oxford: Oxford University Press, 2016.

Whelan, Frederick G. "Prologue: Democratic Theory and the Boundary Problem." *Liberal Democracy* 25 (1983): 13–47.

White, Stephen. "Weak Ontology and Liberal Political Reflection." *Political Theory* 25, no. 4 (August 1997): 502–23.

Wicker, Tom. *A Time to Die*. Chicago: Haymarket Books, 2011.

X, Malcolm. *The Autobiography of Malcolm X (as Told to Alex Haley)*. New York: Random House, 1965.

Young, Iris Marion. *Inclusion and Democracy*. Oxford: Oxford University Press, 2000.

Zimring, Franklin E. *The Insidious Momentum of American Mass Incarceration*. New York: Oxford University Press, 2020.

Zinn, Howard. *Justice in Everyday Life*. Boston: South End Press, 1974.

Index

Abizadeh, Arash, 20
abolition of punishment, 60–61
Abrahams, Joseph, 26*fig*, 27–28, 29–32, 94
administrator as therapist, 33–34
aggregative democrats, 13, 16
all-affected interest principle, 19
American Journal of Psychiatry, 27
Asylums: Essays on the Social Situation of Mental Patients and Other Inmates (Goffman), 25
Attica prison rebellion, 71, 73
authoritarian governance, 16
authoritarian managerialism, 6

Baker, J. E., 49, 52, 53, 56
Banfield, Edward, 50
Barber, Benjamin, 10, 13, 16, 22
Beaumont, Gustave de, 78
Beckett, Katherine, 11
Black admission ward, Howard Hall, 29–32
Black African Nations Toward Unity (BANTU), 72
Black Power movement, 50
Boone, John, 68, 73
Boston Globe, 78
boundary problems: Barber on limits of universal inclusion, 13; constituting the demos, 17–21, 23; Dahl on boundaries as

matter of contract, 16; fixity and, 21–22; incompetence, interpreting and defining, 8, 11, 14–15, 93; porous nature of boundaries, 21. *See also* exclusion thesis

capacity: democratic exclusion and, 15–17, 22–24; franchise capacity, 20, 22; prisoner self-governance, 81, 82–83, 85; use of term, 98n9, 100n7
carceral imagination, 11
Chamberlin, Judi, 45, 47
Charlestown penitentiary, 62–66
Charlestown penitentiary grievance committee, 62–66
children: democratic exclusions and, 13, 100n13; exclusion thesis and, 10, 13, 15, 20; franchise capacity, 20; as special status, 16–17
citizenship, rights of, 17, 101n23, 102n36; constituting the demos, 17–23; habits of citizenship, 42; patient committed to mental hospitals, 26–27, 105nn5–6. *See also* exclusion thesis
civic competence: patient administrative groups and, 38–39; patient federations and, 42–44; role of organizations in, 8; Walpole prisoner self-governance and, 81–83

Olson, Joel, 15
organizational politics, 6
Osborne, Thomas, 2
Overholser, Winfred, 27, 29, 41
Overton window, 6

parens patriae, 4–7
Participation and Democratic Theory (Pateman), 81
participatory democrats, 13, 16
Pateman, Carole, 81, 83, 85, 128n82
patient administrative groups (PAGs), 27; initial formation of, 33–35; mad democracy, 45–47; overview of, 35–40
patient federation, Dorothea Dix Service, 40–44; mad democracy, 45–47
patient self-governance, 25–28; Howard Hall, St. Elizabeths Hospital, 8, 27–28; problem of collective organization, 28–35
Pitts, Jennifer, 13
Piven, Francis, 50
Pound, Ezra, 28
prepolitical claim, democratic exclusion and, 15–17
prisoners: Charlestown penitentiary grievance committee, 62–66; community control in custody, controversy and criticism, 56–61, 91; community in, family resemblance of, 55–56; inmate advisory councils, 64, 65–66; limits of community, 61–62; multilevel grievance procedures, 52–53, 55; prison community, 50–55; prisoner councils, 52–54, 55, 58; prison unions, 54–55, 85–86, 94; rebellions by, 50; theories of punishment, 15; use of term, 97n2. *See also* custody; Walpole prison, Massachusetts
prison labor: prison unions, 9, 54–56, 70, 74, 77, 79, 84, 85–86, 94, 128n79, 128n82; strike of 2016, 86
prisons: Charlestown penitentiary grievance committee, 62–66; community control in, controversy and criticism, 56–61, 91; community in, family resemblance of, 55–56; custodial confinement, advocates and critics of, 1–3; custodial institutions, overview of, 4–7; limits of community, 61–62; multilevel grievance procedures, 52–53, 55; prison as a constitutional government, 78–79; prisoner councils, 52–54; reform efforts, 50–52, 56–61, 65–66, 78–79, 94–95; as sites of civic

renewal, 48–50. *See also* custody; *specific prison names*
The Prison Community (Clemmer), 51
prison unions, 9, 54–56, 70, 74, 77, 79, 84, 85–86, 94, 128n79, 128n82
psychoanalysis, 29
publicity in custody, 9
punishment: abolition of, 60–61; custodial institutions, roles of, 4, 12, 59, 126n61; reform efforts, 82; theories of, 15

qualification, use of term, 100n7

race: Black admission ward, Howard Hall, 29–32; democratic exclusion and, 13–14, 15; ethno-racial conflict within prison community, 72–74, 75, 82; penology of racial innocence, 11; racial caste in America, 84; Walpole, formal structure of self-rule, 74
Raz, Joseph, 19
Reiss, Benjamin, 47
Resident Government Council (RGC), Walla Walla, Washington, 53–54, 58
restorative justice practices, 57, 119n38
Rodman, Ed, 67
Rooney, Larry, 76
Rothman, David, 1, 60, 94–95
Rust, Obalaji, 71

San Francisco county jail, therapeutic community, 3
Sargent, Francis, 73
self-governance, 89; democracy, erosion of, 92–96. *See also* Howard Hall, St. Elizabeths Hospital; Walpole prison, Massachusetts
Serpasil, 44
sex offenders, exclusion of, 82
Shapiro, Ian, 17, 18, 100n13
Shaw, Clifford, 29
Simon, Jonathan, 56–57
Sing-Sing prison, Mutual Welfare League, 2
Skarbek, David, 58
social facts, 21
status, attribution of, 17, 21
St. Elizabeths Hospital, Washington, D.C., 11*fig*, 26*fig*; John Howard Pavilion, 35–36; mad democracy, 45–47; patient administration groups (PAGs), 33–40; patient federations, 40–44; patient self-governance, 8, 25, 27–28, 90–91; problem of collective organization,

Founded in 1893,
UNIVERSITY OF CALIFORNIA PRESS
publishes bold, progressive books and journals
on topics in the arts, humanities, social sciences,
and natural sciences—with a focus on social
justice issues—that inspire thought and action
among readers worldwide.

The UC PRESS FOUNDATION
raises funds to uphold the press's vital role
as an independent, nonprofit publisher, and
receives philanthropic support from a wide
range of individuals and institutions—and from
committed readers like you. To learn more, visit
ucpress.edu/supportus.

www.ingramcontent.com/pod-product-compliance
Lightning Source LLC
Chambersburg PA
CBHW030334270326
41926CB00010B/1627